# Raising Children in a Digital Age

D0654729

*"I am delighted to see this book pulling together the many strands of work which are designed to help parents, carers, children, and young people navigate the online world. Bex is clearly passionate about helping people engage with the digital world in a positive way, and this comes through in the simple discussion pointers in each chapter. Too often a lack of understanding of the opportunities and challenges presented by technological change becomes an excuse for no engagement; Bex points out that this is wrong and that opportunities to engage in really good communication come from getting to grips with this new environment. She sets out some great ways to achieve this."*

**Reg Bailey CBE, Chief Executive
of Mothers' Union**

*"A refreshingly direct and thoughtful guide for parents who want to understand their kids' digital world but don't want to be patronised. Up to date and evidence-based, this book walks a finely-judged line between inviting parents to get involved and trusting kids to be sensible as well as suggesting constructive ways for parents to talk to and also learn from their children."*

**Professor Sonia Livingstone OBE,
London School of Economics, author of *Children
and the Internet***

# RAISING CHILDREN IN A DIGITAL AGE

## ENJOYING THE BEST
## AVOIDING THE WORST

## BEX LEWIS

LION

*For my parents, who have sought to support me through the choices I have made in life.*

Published by Lion Books
an imprint of
**Lion Hudson plc**
Wilkinson House, Jordan Hill Road,
Oxford OX2 8DR, England
www.lionhudson.com/lion

ISBN 978 0 7459 5604 6
e-ISBN 978 0 7459 5755 5

First edition 2014

**Acknowledgments**
p. 11 Picture of Bex Lewis © Keith Blundy

pp. 14, 39–40, 123, 188, 206, 216: Extracts from *The Byron Review* by Professor Tanya Byron © Professor Tanya Byron, 2008. Reproduced with permission.

pp. 40, 60, 123, 126: Extracts from CHILDWISE "Digital Lives" Report © CHILDWISE, 2010. Reproduced with permission.

pp. 36, 109, 142, 166, 170, 197: Extracts from Janna Anderson and Lee Rainie, "Imagining the Internet: Millennials will benefit and suffer due to their hyperconnected lives". Pew Research Center, Washington, D.C. (February 29, 2012). http://www.pewinternet.org/Reports/2012/Hyperconnected-lives.aspx, accessed on February 29, 2012.

pp. 42, 167, 214: Extracts from *Me and My Web Shadow* by Antony Mayfield © Antony Mayfield, 2010, A&C Black, an imprint of Bloomsbury Publishing Plc. Reproduced with permission.

p. 102: Extract from "Randi Zuckerberg: How I Unplug For My Family" by Randi Zuckerberg © Randi Zuckerberg, 2013. Reproduced with permission.

A catalogue record for this book is available from the British Library

Printed and bound in the UK, January 2014, LH26

# Contents

# A Chance to Say Thank You...

… to Ali Hull for first commissioning this book and for encouragement and correction in the editing process, and to Pete Phillips, Andy Byers, Rich Wyld, Penny Bissell, Tim Hutchings, and Kate Bruce (my CODEC team at Durham University) for providing me with links and enthusiastic encouragement.

I've enjoyed the support from my Facebook and Twitter communities, through feedback, suggested links, and distributing the questionnaire. Heartfelt thanks to the 120 anonymous people who replied to it. I've relished feedback from speaking engagements and blog posts that has helped develop the focus and advice within this book, and ongoing encouragement from former colleagues at the University of Winchester, particularly Martin Polley and Joyce Goodman, who developed my capacity for sustained writing with my PhD; Tansy Jessop, who has encouraged the continued development of my writing skills since; and Yaz El-Hakim who afforded many e-learning opportunities.

I've particularly appreciated the opportunities for early chats with Marcus Leaning (Head of Media & Film, University of Winchester), Penny Fuller (Children & Youth Development Officer, Methodist Church), and Maggie Barfield (Children's Publishing List, Scripture Union), and ongoing thought processes with fellow Social Media Consultant Bryony Taylor. I've valued many offline conversations with those in the Cranmer Hall/Wesley Study Centre community – including big hugs from Merry Evans – where many are wrestling with these issues day by day with their own children, in the midst of busy lives.

I also want to thank Leanne and Darren Bell (we first connected on Twitter), who gave me not only a great day out at Alnwick Castle and lots of chats about children and social media, but also the opportunity to observe three children of differing ages engaging with digital media in really positive ways. Siân and Chris Lawton, Jennifer and Andrew Riddlestone, Justine and Matt McNinch, Pen Andrews, Geoff and Helen Hobbs, Jon and Kate Whale and Nicky Robinson have also given me plenty of opportunity to get involved in how they manage their children at work and play both online and offline. Thanks also to Louise Upchurch for the teacher's perspective, and to Paul Windo (Urban Saints) for the youth leader's.

As always, I am grateful to friends and family for support, encouragement, time with nieces and nephews, and time out – especially my parents, who have unfailingly supported, challenged, and encouraged me through good times and bad; my cousin Hannah, who provides great conversation and feedback along with a sofa bed for trips to London; and the Hitchens/Beresfords, who have been my honorary Winchester family for several years (and whose old dishwasher has made the writing process much easier!).

I also want to make a special mention of Tracey Hume, who drove me around to find my new home, and my new neighbours in Durham, Pat and Fred, with their friends John and Ang, who have sought to motivate me by helping me manage my garden, alongside various "Have you finished that book yet?" pokes. These have also been particularly appreciated from Sara Batts (hard-stare specials), Sheridan Voysey, Vicky Walker, Maggi Dawn, Emma Giles, Mary Jackson, Christina Macleod, Karen Neal, Emma Lowe, Melanie Cunningham, Pam Smith, and Paul and Pam Webster – along with ice-pops from Beth Weedon and years of encouragement from Andrew Graystone!

Last, and not least, I ask forgiveness of all those who have chatted with me over the years and whose names I have failed to mention.

I'd love to talk to more of you online, so join me on Twitter (@digitalfprint // @drbexl) with tag #digitalparenting.

# Meet @drbexl

It's late 1992. I've settled down to watch my new (old) television. It's the first television our family possesses (previously forbidden for "misconceived religious reasons", to quote my mum), and I cannot get enough of it. My parents worry that I'm attached to the screen, undiscriminating in what I watch, and losing out on time outside, although I'm enjoying the fact that I can finally join in the school conversations about programmes such as *Neighbours.*

These worries sound familiar, right? After the first buzz of TV ownership, however, I became more discriminating about what I watched, returned to my many books... and was frequently on my bike – I needed it to get to my Saturday job! Having learned to touch-type at secondary school, in 1993 I enjoyed the transition to my mum's word processor in order to write my A-Level dissertation. The summer before heading to university (1994), I spent my entire student loan on my first computer, and at a temp placement I had to send my first email. I still remember the terror and the thrill!

Roll on to 1997. I'm sending emails without even thinking about the platform, and it's time to build my first website! I've just started a PhD studying wartime propaganda posters, and I want the world to know about the discoveries that I'm making. Much of the world now *does* know about my PhD, as it included the history of the *Keep Calm and Carry On* poster (you can read more at http://ww2poster.co.uk). That was the first of many websites and the beginning of a real appetite for understanding what's possible online. I went on to teach media studies, specialized in e-learning, and observed how many university students were *not* the fabled "digital natives".

Having gained so much from it myself, I am very passionate about helping people to engage with the digital world in a positive way, including my nephews and nieces – both blood relations and the many to whom I am an honorary auntie. Having encouraged teenagers to get involved when I was working as a Guide leader, having worked with abandoned street children in Brazil, and having taken responsibility for my friends' children on a regular basis, I'm always keen to balance opportunities with responsibility. If I took any of those children swimming, I'd check that they could swim or had armbands if necessary. In the same way, before sending a child online, I'd check to see whether they had any previous experience, and what support they needed.

My formal job is as Research Fellow in Social Media and Online Learning, and Director of The BIGBible Project for CODEC (Centre for Christian Communication in a Digital Age), based at St John's College, Durham University. I am also the Director of Digital Fingerprint, a social media consultancy whose clients include the Church of England, the United Reformed Church, the Methodist Church, the JISC (Joint Information Systems Committee), and universities, notably focusing on "Social Media for the Scared". I frequently speak at conferences and events, and appear regularly in the press.

# Introduction:
# What Am I Going to
# Gain from this Book?

"Four-year-old girl is Britain's youngest iPad ADDICT: Shocking rise in children hooked on using smartphones and tablets"
**Daily Mail, April 2013**

"Schoolgirl hangs herself after she's bullied by online trolls"
**Metro, April 2013**

"Parents told to beware children running up huge bills on iPad and iPhone game apps"
**The Guardian, January 2013**

"Stop porn on the net corrupting adolescents' idea of sex"
**The Sun, February 2013**

"Nearly half admit to using phones and computers to communicate with people in the same house"
**ITV, February 2013**

"Common Sense Media Polls Finds Fear of Violence Running High"
**The Escapist, January 2013**

"Study: Kids Who Watch 3+ Hours of TV More Likely to Lie, Cheat Later"
*The Atlantic*, **March 2013**

"For Children, a Lie on Facebook Has Consequences, Study Finds"
*The New York Times*, **November 2012**

"Sleep Texting Is On The Rise, Experts Suggest"
*The Huffington Post*, **February 2013**

"30% of teen girls take few precautions meeting men on web"
**CBC News, January 2013**

Are you baffled, confused, scared or terrified by such headlines, which appear with great regularity in our press?

In 2008, Professor Tanya Byron, a well-known psychologist, produced a significant policy review for the UK government entitled "Safer Government in a Digital World", which she revisited in 2010. She acknowledged that there had been increased media debate about the subject, but claimed that too much "still predominantly focuses on the extreme, often tragic, and thankfully rare cases of harm to children and young people" as she called for reporters to report in a balanced way to better reflect the wide range of experiences online.[1]

**EXERCISE: Take time to think about the news stories you've seen in recent weeks. What are they focusing on? Are they seeking to scare or to support?**

CHILDWISE, a UK research agency that provides insights into children's use of, and attitudes to, media, has produced annual reports since 1991, drawing on a network of over 1,000 schools. In 2010 they did a special report, "Digital Lives", which looked particularly at confident child users online and which highlighted that engaging with the digital environment is not optional, as in reality "few interests or activities exist exclusively, or even predominantly, outside its influence".[2] The longer we live with the "new media", the more it becomes just "media".

As those who care for children, we need to understand the realities of the situation online, to ensure that debates about child digital safety are balanced with an understanding of how children truly engage with the digital spaces, and an appreciation of the benefits of digital engagement. We'll draw on a range of stories highlighted by these headlines throughout the book, considering which are worth paying attention to, and which need debunking, while also looking at some of the challenges from history that will help dissipate our fears.

## Should we truly be fearful?

For newspapers, "fear sells": it grabs our attention and encourages us to read the stories. Many of the risks we are likely to encounter are small and easily addressed, but they are not new or glamorous and so tend not to attract press, and therefore politicians', attention. As Pamela Whitby, a journalist, says:

*The press have a habit of scaremongering parents and hyping the online risks to our children out of all proportion. Often articles are poorly researched and people are regularly misquoted. Numbers are bandied about which at first glance appear shocking, but dig a little deeper and you quickly start to understand what sells newspapers.[3]*

We need to remember that newspapers love "averages", and that a few heavy users can affect the overall statistics: a child who is online over ten hours a day distorts figures that would otherwise show two hours a day, causing panic about childhood screen addiction. Dan Gardner, another journalist, believes this is such a problem that we are directing attention and money to the wrong issues, and therefore not focusing on the subjects that we really ought to be. We also need to understand that correlations in data don't necessarily imply causation – just because people who play video games can be aggressive doesn't mean that video gaming causes aggression. Those who are naturally aggressive may be attracted to particular types of video game, or there may be other factors involved.[4]

This book is designed to equip you to help your children enjoy digital media safely, and focus on the areas where *you* can make a difference. As Rebecca Levey, an educational and technology journalist, emphasizes in *Mashable*, the core site for social media news: "You are the parent, and a screen doesn't change that."[5] As you would when helping them learn to ride a bike, find out as much as you can about the digital environment so that you can enjoy it safely with your children.

Many of the topics that we will look at in this book are relevant to all age groups: whatever capacity we are in, we are role models for other users online. There is so much poor information out there. This book seeks out the quality information, making academic research digestible, and combines it with my years of experience in engaging in digital culture, to help give you confidence as a parent online as well as offline.

As a university lecturer and e-learning specialist, I have observed first-hand the real social benefits of digital media for students new to university. Social networks such as Facebook help them to integrate more quickly with their new community, while also having the support of their old community online.

As the digital environment can change so fast, any book of this nature may appear to be but a snapshot in time, but many of the social platforms that we use have been around for quite a while, and everything that you learn now will help you as other social platforms evolve. This book will focus particularly on the underlying principles of online engagement, while also offering practical advice where appropriate. There are particular issues that we need to be aware of with children, and these will be highlighted. I also recognize that you are the expert on parenting – this is but another area in which you need to be equipped with knowledge so you can parent effectively in the online environment.

## Who is responsible?

Western cultures emphasize individual responsibility, and parents certainly have to fulfil their obligations, but we also need to think about what we as a society, including politicians and industry, can do to help make this job easier. Responsibility for children's positive online engagement cannot be solely down to parents, and research demonstrates that children are learning from a wide variety of sources, including family, friends, teachers, school staff, youth leaders, advertising, print media, and a range of spaces online.

Although many parents think that the internet is regulated, the 2008 Byron Review emphasized that we can't rely purely on any government to protect our children. The internet is a global phenomenon, and "there is no obvious single point at which editorial control can be exercised". Professor Byron called for a parental shift in attitudes from assuming "somebody must be doing something to regulate the Internet", or allowing themselves to feel powerless, to understanding the importance of their role in ensuring child safety online.

Note that Byron is calling for *all* adults to take responsibility. Antony Mayfield, a digital strategist, gives a helpful analogy: in the Italian mountains, everyone has responsibility for clearing snow from their area. If they sat back and waited for government gritting lorries, they would all be stuck for weeks.[6] In the same way, online we are all citizens of the web: with such opportunities come responsibilities, not just for ourselves but also for others in the online community.

## Questionnaire

Working within social media, I decided to crowd-source online some material specific to this book, designing a short and simple questionnaire[7] and asking those in my networks who have responsibility for childcare to complete it and also pass it on to friends. Over the course of a month, I received 120 responses covering the key opportunities and fears that people have about going online, the practices they have in place to ensure digital safety, and any further insights that respondents wanted to offer.

Given the title of the questionnaire, it was no surprise that responses were mostly from parents, although others came from aunts, uncles, grandparents, other family members, and carers. The age range of children covered everything from birth to nineteen+. The age options given were: "2 or under; 3 to 5; 6 to 9; 10 to 12; 13 to 15; 16 to 18; and 19 or over". Significant numbers had children across a range of age groups, with the largest numbers being in the six- to nine-year-old age group. These quotes will appear throughout the book as below:

• • • • • • • • • • • • • • • • • • • • • • • • • • • • • • • • • •

I think fear is often whipped up by the popular press… Simple guidelines for parents on how to use the internet safeguards they already have would perhaps be helpful, as well as clear and calm reporting that does not panic people into seeing a huge threat that isn't there and a problem that is insurmountable. I know I'm asking for the world…

**(Parent, 3 to 5)**

Given also that the questionnaire was conducted digitally, it's unsurprising that over a hundred of the respondents were "Comfortable" or "Entirely Happy" with their own confidence online. This confidence, however, although not disappearing entirely, dropped significantly when it came to allowing their children to engage digitally.

**Navigating this book**

This book is intended to give you that confidence! It starts with a bit of history to show that the issues you're facing are not new, a section on digital culture to help you understand what's particular about it, and some practical advice on the current significant tools. It then moves on to more practical advice, tips, and tricks with regard to particular areas of significance, and finally looks at specific advice for grandparents, teachers, and youth leaders, while also putting a futurology hat on. You then have the opportunity to take your learning further by means of a range of resources listed at the back of the book.

I hope that you enjoy the book and find that it builds your online confidence, and enables you to support safe and positive experiences for your children (and others) online.

# 1

# Challenging Fears:
# Brief Lessons from History

· · · · · · · · · · · · · · · · · · · · · · · · · · · · · · ·

Don't be scared, don't be fearful; just be aware and help your children to navigate this phase of life.
**(Parent, 13 to 15, 16 to 18)**

Emma Mulqueeny, chief executive of Rewired State, the UK's largest independent developer network, said that "a culture of caution" means children are being taught to fear the internet rather than understand it.[1] We want to confront those fears, and one way to place our modern anxieties in perspective is to look to history. As Media Studies lecturer Marcus Leaning writes, "Numerous studies indicate how daily life will be transformed or improved through use of the Internet", but it is also seen as a threat. The "terrifying possibilities of new technologies" are not unique to the internet.[2] The journalist Dan Gardner, in his 2008 book *Risk,* declared that although all generations have faced risk, ours is the most terrified. History demonstrates that there have always been doom-mongers, particularly in the press, but we are "the healthiest, wealthiest, and longest-lived people in history. And we are increasingly afraid. This is one of the great paradoxes of our time."[3]

With every new technological advance, including the printing press, the telephone, and the television, fears have been raised. These are known as "moral panics". Frank Furedi, a sociologist, suggests that these occur when society feels unable to adapt to dramatic changes and fears a loss of control. This is not helped by the fact that the media tend to generalize from single instances of harm, implying that we are all "at risk".

Another phrase that's worth introducing to your vocabulary is "technological determinism": a sense that each new form of technology comes with new ways of doing things, in which we have no say. It is more helpful to understand that all new technologies come with new possibilities for ways of doing things, some good and some bad, and that we have choices about how we put them to use: whether that form of technology is the Biro, a watch, an iPad, a rocket, or a nuclear bomb.

In focusing on these "moral panics" and believing that "technological determinism" is in place, we may concentrate our efforts on the wrong "solutions", to the detriment of our children. We know that both technology and media play significant roles in our lives, but there are other factors, including cultural and economic, that also need consideration. Nancy Willard, the director of the Center for Safe and Responsible Internet Use, agrees that the fears regularly aired in the media are "disproportionate to the [research] data or the actual degree of risk". These fears are overhyped by those with products to sell to parents, such as filtering software, and by law enforcement agencies, whose default position is to focus on fear as they see the worst cases, but who are often brought into schools to teach children about online safety.[4]

```
I believe there is a lot of misinformation and
scaremongering, but the risks are also very real.
```
**(Parent, 3 to 5, 6 to 9)**

The Pew Internet Research Center in the USA produces regular reports on aspects of American life online. Their 2012 report, "Future of the Internet", which sought opinions from over a thousand technology professionals, provided several positive responses to these fears.[5] US communications consultant Stowe Boyd noted that our concerns will look old-fashioned in a decade, in the same way that Socrates feared the introduction of the written language, and parents feared Elvis Presley's rock-and-roll dance moves. We'll stop "seeing" technology, and it will just be. Jessica Clark, a media strategist and senior fellow for two US communications technology research centres, is similarly positive:

*History is a progression of older people tut-tutting over the media production and consumption habits of those younger than them and holding tightly to the belief that the technologies of communication they grew up with are intellectually or culturally superior.*

We each find new ways to use technology for good and for bad. We will find ways to live with it, and life will go on, and we should be aware that countries that can afford technology tend to have more resources to manage its risks.

## The development of a "risk" society

Although it is the early enthusiasts who bring us new technologies, it is only once the general population looks past the risks and sees the potential for everyday application that technologies go mainstream. Didn't we all laugh at the idea of owning a mobile phone, and don't we now all check "wallet, phone, keys"?

So, is it the continuous negative coverage of digital media in the mainstream media that contributes to negative perceptions, and, if so, how do we address that? Back to Dan Gardner and *Risk*, and a telling examp le: after 9/11 people were fearful of travelling by plane, so hundreds more Americans took to the roads. Statistics show that this resulted in 5,000 more road deaths than would be expected for a normal year. But whereas a plane crash attracts significant press attention, road deaths do not – each is written off as an "unfortunate accident".[6] We need to understand which fears are constructive, and act upon them, and which are "unreasoning fears" or "moral panics". Gardner says that "the paedophile lurking in parks and Internet chat rooms" comes into this category.[7] In the past, we could say that children were expected to take knocks and chances as a part of growing up, with risk taking seen as a necessary part of child development. Now, risk has become something to be avoided at all costs, and this attitude is fuelled by media stories.

The spectres of dangers are often developed from the media that we consume, whether that be press, films (when we're in a more relaxed mode), or online material. So, does that mean we can't win, whatever we do? By 2008 Professor Byron agreed that the "range of risks is reaching a stage of consensus", but what is not clear is the actual harm that we fear from risks. For example, does pornography harm children now, or does it affect their longer-term sexual development? Or does it simply take their innocence away? If we can articulate more clearly what we fear, then we can start to deal with those fears.

Byron also wants parents to consider that what we view as a risk may also present new opportunities, such as making new friends from online contacts. Risk does not automatically mean harm, so we need to be careful about when and how we intervene, to ensure that children are encouraged to engage positively online rather than fear the digital spaces.

Hanna Rosin, writing in *The Atlantic*, and noting that we have become risk-averse and now decry failure, quotes from Frank and Theresa Caplan's 1973 book *The Power of Play*, questioning what puts one student ahead of another:

*Certainly it is more than verbal skill. To create, one must have a sense of adventure and playfulness. One needs toughness to experiment and hazard the risk of failure. One has to be strong enough to start all over again if need be and alert enough to learn from whatever happens. One needs a strong ego to be propelled forward in one's drive toward an untried goal. Above all, one has to possess the ability to play![8]*

The Canadian not-for-profit organization MediaSmarts report in 2012 reflected back to 2000, when they first talked to children. At this point children had seen the internet as a private space that adults couldn't enter or control. Therefore, what they did online was "consequence-free". By 2004, technology was fully integrated into their social lives: they were able to try on different identities, deepen relationships with offline friends, and engage in their passions. As time moved on, identity was becoming more important as a way to connect, so going online was less anonymous, but children started to develop their own text language as a battle back against monitoring:

*In 2011, that private space for play had mostly disappeared. Our participants told us that the Internet is now a fully monitored space where parents, teachers and corporations keep them under constant surveillance.[9]*

Talking of surveillance, COPPA (the Children's Online Privacy Protection Act) came into effect on 1 July 2013. It is US-based, but designed for a global world and affects what other nations do – and stipulates that any social network knowingly collecting information from children must ask their parents' consent.[10]

## Changing families

Alongside technological changes, we need to consider the other elements of our lives that have changed in order to understand how some of our fears have originated. A significant change is in family life: we have fewer marriages and more divorce, separation, and cohabitation. More children are born outside marriage, they stay at home longer, we get married and have children later in life, and generally people live longer. Vodafone's 2010 research highlights how family life is both more privatized (as parents focus on their own children rather than on wider society), and yet also open to much wider influences through the constant presence of technology:

> *Children's place in the family and society has been transformed from the "seen and not heard" of past generations to the centre of family life. Their ability to influence major family decisions and their purchasing power has been noted by companies.[11]*

Within the family, notions of childhood have changed, and we need to beware of romanticizing our own childhoods, when we "ran free in the streets", as if danger didn't exist while we were growing up. Before a 24/7 news culture, hungry to fill news slots, maybe the dangers didn't look as fearsome. In the past, society tended to see children as inherently naughty, requiring discipline, whereas now they are perceived as inherently good, with an innocence that can be corrupted and requires protection. The way we deal with children has further changed as the market has developed a range of new classifications for children: the "teenager" in the 1950s, and more recently the "tweenager", "middle youth", "kidult", and "adultescent", changing the way we perceive children and their needs, and how we think others are treating their children.

As children are increasingly given access to a global world through mass media, they are being increasingly controlled, regulated, and surveyed. Despite valuing their spontaneity and imagination, as parents we increasingly control and organize their lives,[12] and feel pressured to give them a "good" childhood with opportunities for success as an adult, while protecting them from both physical and social risks. Some children, however, will return to empty homes where computers and mobile devices offer a range of communities for them to participate in while family members are absent.

. . . . . . . . . . . . . . . . . . . . . . . . . . . . . . . . . . . . . .

I work outside the home and although my husband works from home, the business is at a crucial stage and therefore it is not always easy for him to supervise the children very closely until I return from work; which normally leaves a window of one and a half hours in which the children at times absorb themselves in the Xbox, the mobile phone or the TV.

**(Parent, 6 to 9, 13 to 15)**

## Common fears

Between 2009 and 2011, the London School of Economics and its research partners interviewed over 25,000 children and their parents across twenty-five countries in Europe in the "EU Kids Online Project".[13] This study found that children were most commonly afraid of cyberbullying and insults online, visual pornography, meeting with strangers, and seeing something violent, while child abuse, paedophilia, "fake things", and drug-based websites were also mentioned.

One of the purposes of my questionnaire was to establish what parents are concerned about, so that this book could be written to provide practical resources to build confidence in dealing with their concerns. There was a wide range, including the big things we see in the press: "stranger danger"; accessing porn; cyberbullying; addiction; ID theft; loss of social abilities; and the lack of control that parents feel over their children's use of technology because it is increasingly mobile. Parents worry about the tools available to them, finding filtering software too complicated or inefficient and the technology giants too powerful to engage with. Other concerns included what children post online, the pressure to conform in order to be popular, oversharing, the lack of criticality, the public nature of disagreements, the speed at which messages spread, and the "digital footprint" (the digital trail left by all online activities and interactions) that children are creating for their future.

Parents were also worried about a lack of sociability because children don't spend time with "real people", information overload, a lack of focus, impatience, poor-quality English triggered by overuse of grammatically poor, misspelt "textspeak", and the fact that, with no time to be bored, creativity was being stifled. Some were concerned that, in a consumerist world, we are all being pressurized into buying the latest devices (thus making us a target for mugging), and the resulting focus on individualism leads to a lack of concern for the wider community. Some were afraid that children are spending too much time viewing screens, a distraction from "more rewarding pastimes" such as time outside, with potential damage to their eyesight and hearing, and the danger of children acquiring a "skewed view of the world" from the unreliable information they read online.

> **EXERCISE: Take at least fifteen minutes, with your child (if they're old enough), to identify a list of fears you/they have, so that you can start to tick them off as you work through this book.**

## Looking hopeful?

I want to get across to parents that I have huge and positive expectations for the way technology will continue to enhance our lives, and the lives of the coming generations. The research I have come across backs up this view. Jeana Lee Tahnk, who writes the Screen Play technology blog for *Parenting* magazine, comments that technology has made her more organized. She now benefits from a phone diary, and can take photos to save her children's "artwork" that would otherwise be "gently removed" from the fridge for the bin. Her GPS has reduced the stress of driving around, and it has become easier to share memories and photos, to maintain contact with family via Skype, to organize quick play dates at the last minute by texting, and, in particular, to deal with all the how/why questions by Googling everything.[14]

I asked my questionnaire respondents what they thought were the benefits of the digital world, and their answers included access to a wide range of information (especially if not blocked by a filter), increased connection with family/friends regardless of distance, huge educational benefits for the future, giving children an opportunity to engage with the world as it is now, opportunities to demonstrate – and be involved in – collaboration, a positive impact on social life, the opportunity to make more flexible plans, tools to keep children occupied, a chance to enjoy spending time together on devices and to learn from their children, the global nature of the online spaces, fun and entertainment, learning from games, improved hand–eye co-ordination, the speed of communication, learning to be critical, enhanced personal safety, increased accessibility for those with disabilities, and prospects for increased creativity.

**EXERCISE: Take at least fifteen minutes, with your child (if they're old enough), to discuss the positive potential you can see in the internet, and identify something new to try.**

Before we move on to addressing the particular fears that many parents and others have regarding children and the digital world, first let's look at its value.

# 2

# Digital Culture:
# Why It Matters that We Join In

Before we move on to specific aspects of digital culture, let's think about why we should all be involved in it, and what its benefits are. Professor Tanya Byron, author of the Byron Report (2008), said: "I found the more that I understood what [my children] were experiencing, the more I felt empowered to support them to [go online] responsibly and safely, and the more freedom I felt comfortable for them to have."[1] As one questionnaire respondent said:

. . . . . . . . . . . . . . . . . . . . . . . . . . . . . . . . . . . . .

Digital is there and will only increase, so it's good to work with [our children] about appropriate usage while we can still wield some influence.
**(Parent, 13 to 15)**

Throughout history, children have always consumed different types of media. If you're worried about threats, the best response is to understand what they are. If you're not already using digital technology, start using it and get to understand what helps online and what doesn't, and regain the ability to make informed choices. If you're already online, explore the sites your children are involved in. You don't need to be a digital "expert" (if there's any such thing) to keep yourself and your family safe online. None of us know it all, and don't believe the media hype that says that children do know it all, with parents left way behind. The more we can understand online cultures (and each is slightly different), the better we can help our children engage with them productively.

• • • • • • • • • • • • • • • • • • • • • • • • • • • • • • • • • • • • •

Many parents lack confidence in the use of modern technology, some don't have regular access to these resources and are therefore unable to supervise or even be aware of what their children might, or might not, be getting up to online.

**(Parent, 13 to 15)**

• • • • • • • • • • • • • • • • • • • • • • • • • • • • • • • • • • • • •

I am very glad that both my husband and I are relatively comfortable with digital technology but I still feel that it is increasingly challenging to ensure that children use digital technology appropriately.

**(Parent, 2 or under)**

*A useful video that uses the data from the European research (2010) to visualize what children do online can be found at: http://www. niceandserious.com/portfolio-item/liberty-global-the-digital-universe/*

Social networks now make it easy to contribute online, making online spaces accessible to a much larger number of people who would never have had the technical skill or interest to undertake this through a personal website. And having so many friends, family, and business acquaintances already on social networks provides a reason for all of us to be online.

> We don't have any major fears because we've taken the
> time from early on to set boundaries on what he does,
> and expectations of how he does it. We started with
> limiting TV time, never having a TV/computer in the
> bedroom, and taking the mickey out of the stupid ads
> on TV! He knows we know how to go back through his
> search history on the computer, so no problems there.
> It would be out of character for him to do anything
> dodgy on his touch or phone, both of which are hand-
> me-downs so not state-of-the-art or expensive kit. He
> also knows that the privilege of use would be revoked
> if he messed up — so he hasn't ;-)
>
> **(Parent, 16 to 18)**

The "digital revolution" has affected all our lives, whether we are proactively engaged or not. Every time you shop in the supermarket, take public transport, or search on Google, data is collected about you. Social media commentators such as Erik Qualman[2] highlight the numbers active on social networks and how online activity is now as mundane as using the phone. There are over 1 billion active users on Facebook, 500 million on Google+, and 300 million on Twitter. YouTube users upload around seventy-two hours of video per minute, and people are increasingly sharing photos, videos, and status updates on a variety of other social media platforms.

Children can find the internet exciting, as everything, both good and bad, is available to them. Their online attitudes are similar to their offline ones: innocent curiosity, determination, being either responsible or rebellious. The online world is not a "virtual world". There are real people behind the keyboards at either end of any online activity (for good and for bad), and the activities themselves can be only too real, so we need to ensure that children understand that what they are dealing with offers huge potential for both healthy and corrupt activities. We need to engage with and empower young people for the frequent times when they will be without adult supervision so that they have the tools to remain safe, in particular highlighting what others are doing that is good, and encouraging effective problem solving.

· · · · · · · · · · · · · · · · · · · · · · · · · · · · · · · · · · · ·

At the moment my kids are at an age when my own knowledge of digital tools far outweighs theirs. However, I am worried about the time arriving (fairly soon, I suspect) when this situation is reversed. I think the main concern will be me trying to keep up with them. After all, you cannot police what you are not aware of.
**(Parent, 2 or under, 6 to 9)**

So, what are the *particular* characteristics of digital culture? Digital material is both more ephemeral and more permanent than previous communication methods. It can be difficult to remove and it is easy to change, replicate, and share, which makes it difficult to distinguish between originals and their replicas. What the community chooses to highlight may not be what the author intended, and material can be disseminated fast, but this also means that a response can be made more quickly. Users can have a sense of being invisible, which can lead to irresponsible behaviour, but can also provide the anonymity necessary to encourage someone to engage with online support sites. We should remember, however, that with a little work, anyone can be found and identified. In digital culture people tend to engage with increasing numbers of "friends": it can be harder to detect possible risk, but those with "unique interests" can find friends more easily online.[3]

### The need for "digital literacy"
I've spent the last handful of years working on projects funded by the JISC (Joint Information Systems Committee), who define

"digital literacy" as "those capabilities which fit an individual for living, learning and working in a digital society: for example, the skills to use digital tools to undertake academic research, writing and critical thinking; as part of personal development planning; and as a way of showcasing achievements".[4] Literacy skills have always been important. With the digital environment being so all-consuming, our children need to be critical, constructive, and confident inhabitants of it, to give them the best opportunities to participate in life.

Users need to understand what has been made possible by the introduction of each new form of technology, and what has been limited in order to use the technology well. Think, for example, of the microphone, which allows me to talk to large numbers of people at once, but makes it more difficult for me to speak to any one member of the audience privately. At e-learning conferences we often mention that when paper was first introduced, it was probably seen as disruptive (as users can doodle while a speaker is talking), but we have learned about and adapted to such developments, and we can do the same with digital technologies. Note, however, that just because a tool was designed for one purpose, that doesn't determine what we can do with it. Think of text messages on phones: they were a side product and now are used more frequently than voice calls.

Digital literacy, however, is about far more than knowing how to use the tools; it's about understanding how to access, organize, evaluate, use, and share digitally produced or available information, safely, legally, and creatively.

### Technology: "The bad guy"?

We may, then, accept that we all need to be digitally literate, but we still need to be aware of the challenges that accompany the use of this technology. These include (but are not limited to) the finances required to purchase and maintain it, the batteries it needs (which can be an environmental hazard), the learning required to use the tool well, its effect on productivity at work (usually down to poor regulation of time), concerns in schools such as inattention, cheating, inappropriate pictures, and damage to creativity/imagination, and finally the technology's potential impact on health. In all these cases, and more, are we looking in the right direction for the solution – in other words, is there a problem with the technology itself, or with the choices people make in using it?

As we've seen, the press tends to focus on a range of particular fears, including questions of anonymity, addiction, the 24/7 nature of technology, the loss of verbal cues, the breakdown of social relationships, and other thoughts that would have most parents whisking devices out of their children's hands before you could finish the sentence. We need, however, to remember that good news rarely makes the news, and however unbiased journalists might claim to be, they are stationed only at particular places, on the lookout only for specific types of event, which tend *not* to be the norm.

If we are considering the under-reported benefits of technology, think back to the London riots of 2011. The news was full of how Twitter and BlackBerry® messages were used to organize the riots, with much less attention paid to how that same technology was used to organize the clean-up operation. An article on the BBC highlights how the media changed the message with the selective nature of the tweets that they reported, and that there was much more talk than action.[5] The news reports can provoke a sense of panic, fuelling calls for increased control through laws, zero tolerance, and disciplinary policies in schools, none of which are helpful in encouraging anyone to engage positively with technology. We need to remember, however, that the risks that tend to be highlighted in newspaper headlines have often been accompanied by new ways of solving the problem. Bullying, for example, may now follow children beyond the school gates, but electronic messages can be recorded as "proof" and used as evidence, enabling parents and teachers to deal more effectively with the problem.[6]

Technology is neutral – it can be used for good and bad ends. Martin D. Owens, a US lawyer and author of *Internet Gaming Law*, sums this up nicely in the Pew 2012 report on "Hyper-connected lives":

> *Good people do good things with their access to the Internet and social media – witness the profusion of volunteer and good cause apps and programs which are continually appearing, the investigative journalism, the rallying of pro-democracy forces across the world. Bad people do bad things with their Internet access. Porno access is all over the place – if you want it. Even Al Qaeda has a webpage, complete with interactive social games with a terrorist bent like Make a Bomb in the Kitchen of Your Mom. Just as with J.R.R. Tolkien's ring of power, the Internet grants power to the individual according to that individual's wisdom and moral stature. Idiots are free to do idiotic things with it; the wise are free to acquire more wisdom. It was ever thus. Each new advance in knowledge and technology represents an increase in power, and the corresponding moral choices that go with that power.[7]*

## Focus on the positive

There is a real danger of allowing the darker side of technology to overshadow the wide range of positive opportunities it offers for children's online use. There is then a huge risk of children missing out on technology's benefits because our own fears or lack of knowledge block them from using it.

So what specific benefits does digital technology provide for children? It allows them (and their parents) to undertake a range of tasks: they can communicate instantly with each other, search for information, play games, and make travel arrangements.

Later, it can help them search for jobs. When a club or after-school activity is finished, children can ring or text parents to say that they are done. They can share experiences via phone cameras, and find something to do if bored. Taking part in conversations with others around the globe both widens their knowledge and challenges their cultural stereotypes. The internet has given some children a voice through online projects, encouraged involvement in politics,[8] and raised awareness of substance abuse prevention. Texting can allow more time to think about a message before sending it. At educational conferences, I frequently hear about the ways that digital technology has improved classroom practices. For instance, when Duke University became an Apple Partner for the iPod in 2003, it had no educational application: they let the students determine possible uses. A wide range of suggestions were made, including an audio library of heart rhythms for medical students to learn from.

. . . . . . . . . . . . . . . . . . . . . . . . . . . . . . . . . .

> Parents need to spend time with their children getting to know the services and sites they enjoy using. This allows parents to highlight potential problems, and to guide their child. Technology is not bad, and it can't fix social problems, but technology used responsibly can have a massively positive effect on children.
>
> **(Parent/School IT manager, 6 to 9, 10 to 12)**

### Improving social skills

In 2012 the US agency Common Sense Media produced a report entitled "Social Media, Social Life: How Teens View Their Digital Lives".[9] It quoted some encouraging statistics, which highlighted that more than a quarter of teens say that using their social networking site makes them feel less shy and more outgoing. Other benefits included improved confidence, popularity, and sympathy for others, at the same time as making them feel better about themselves. In addition, a majority of teens said social media helped them keep in touch with friends they couldn't see regularly, get to know other students at their school better, and connect with new people who shared common interests. Parenting specialist Elaine Halligan of The Parent Practice points out:

> *Children will get a sense of community through social networking. And Skype and Twitter provide easy, cheap ways to stay in touch. Children can share ideas, music and photos – which may give them the feeling of making a contribution to debate and discussion.*[10]

## The benefits of digital technology for those with special needs

Many parents or others who work with or care for children with special needs of all kinds may not be aware of the range of benefits digital technology can provide for this sector of society. In 2001–2002 I studied usability and accessibility online, and concluded that what is good for those requiring accessibility is good for all. Sherry Turkle, a US academic with a particular interest in human–technology interaction, noted in 1995 that

> *the opportunities that ICT offers users to access information and communicate with whom they want, freed from the material and social constraints of their bodies, identities, communities and geographies mean that those technologies are regarded as potentially liberating for those who are socially, materially or physically disadvantaged.*[11]

I was therefore surprised to see in the Oxford Internet Institute (OXIS) report "Next Generation Users: The Internet in Britain 2011" that only 41 per cent of those with a disability used the internet, compared with 78 per cent of the non-disabled, especially as there are many stories of technology opening up access.[12] There are, of course, a wide range of disabilities, each requiring different (often expensive) software, although it doesn't have to be complicated:[13]

. . . . . . . . . . . . . . . . . . . . . . . . . . . . . . . . . . . . .

I am the parent of an autistic child, and mobile phones let her have far more independence, as she could ring for help any time.

**(Parent, 19 or over)**

. . . . . . . . . . . . . . . . . . . . . . . . . . . . . . . . . . . . .

All access needs to be controlled by parents but there are some positive aspects to it especially for children who may have special educational needs, i.e. Kindle/iPad for a visually impaired child, as you can select a font size, and a laptop for writing for a child with dyspraxia.

**(Grandparents, 2 or under, 3 to 5)**

. . . . . . . . . . . . . . . . . . . . . . . . . . . . . . . . . . . . .

My younger daughter has Asperger's syndrome, so her use of the internet is rather different... she can be very intense so we have had to pay particular attention to how she uses the 'net. Please be aware of the additional danger for those who are unable to moderate themselves.

**(Parent, 16 to 18)**

This encouraging story was included in the Children's Call for Evidence in the 2008 Byron Review:

*I'm a sufferer of Asperger's syndrome, and video games may have realistically saved my life. I've always had problems talking to people face to face, and was never able to make friends at school. If it weren't for the relationships I formed*

*online through my first games, I honestly can't be sure that
I would be here today [...] they're obviously a great pastime,
which helps me nurture the better side of my syndrome,
thinking and responding logically. As with video gaming, the
Internet helped me form relationships that I couldn't in real life.*

## Online/Offline

So, if we accept that using digital technology is important and can be beneficial to all of us, what else do we need to realize? One vital point is that we're talking about online/offline relationships rather than virtual/real relationships, as though they were completely different. In fact, relationships online may have a different nature, but they are as valid and real as offline relationships. Simply put, most people relate to each other in a variety of ways – face to face, by phone, via email, via Facebook, via text, and even on paper. Our relationships are not usually split into online and virtual relationships, and offline and "real" relationships – and even those that are solely online are no less real than those conducted face to face.

Nor should these relationships have different rules. John Carr, an advisor to the UK government and the UN on child online safety, highlights that the internet is part of everyday life and parents should "teach their children to apply the same values, attitudes and moral behaviour online as they do in the real world".[14] The CHILDWISE "Digital Lives" Report (2010) showed that the children they interviewed felt

*... the online world is no more dangerous or exposed than the
real world, and some believe that the virtual world is actually
more secure and private, because there is more control over
what they choose to put onto the Internet.*

This is echoed by other digital commentators, such as Tom Chatfield:

*This is not to say that I'm the same person online as I am in the flesh. However, the best criteria for judging my experience are precisely those I would apply to most other social experiences and interactions to my life: how much I managed to learn or to communicate; how emotionally connected I felt to others; how enriched the rest of my life was by my interactions.*[15]

One of the main benefits of digital technology is that people are using it to improve their local connections as well as their distant ones, by augmenting them with a digital layer. The OXIS 2011 report demonstrated how the internet had influenced relationships with friends and family, significantly increasing contact with friends both near and far. The internet may be increasing contact with all kinds of people, both similar and different, in contrast to popular notions of creating a virtual "echo chamber", in which everyone listens only to those who think the same way that they do.

If we think about what defines a "community", Wikipedia says it is a group of interacting people living in some proximity (i.e. in space, time, or relationship), a social unit larger than a household, who share common values and have social cohesion.[16] It is far more than a simple geographical entity.

**EXERCISE: Bearing in mind that we are looking for values that work offline as well as online, have a discussion and get your child to draw up a list of the top ten values that they want to demonstrate online (e.g. honesty, friendliness, etc.). If they are keen, consider a list of behaviour to avoid as well, and the consequences of engaging in those negative practices.**

Digital strategist Antony Mayfield offers a really interesting concept – that we often think of the web as a "digital Narnia", a place we don't all need to engage with. He believes we would be better off thinking of the digital environment more in terms of Harry Potter:

> *There are places that are apart from the world, but mostly it exists all around us, simply out of sight to the uninitiated. That leaves a lot of people feeling like Muggles, then. Worse, Muggles who get glimpses of what the digerati are up to. What to do? Ignore them? Rally against them? Or pick up a wand and see what happens?* [17]

The web has increasingly become a layer over our physical world, augmenting our ability to make the most of it. So, if we're going to make the best use of this layer, let's look at some of the current options in our toolkit.

*There are plenty of examples across the net of children using technology in creative ways, often inspired by personal incidents in their lives:*

- *In response to a friend's suicide, a teenager set up a Twitter account giving compliments to others online: http://mashable. com/2013/05/04/sweet-compliments-twitter*
- *In response to bullying at school, another child set up a Twitter account to provide positive comments about others across the school: http://www.cleveland.com/bay-village/index. ssf/2013/05/bay_high_school_senior_lauded.html*
- *In Manchester, after-school Code Clubs are running: http:// www.manchestereveningnews.co.uk/news/greater-manchester-news/talking-digital-teaching-manchesters-children-4750001*
- *A child developed a high-capacity battery with fast recharge: http://mashable.com/2013/05/22/super-capacitor-eesha-khare/*
- *Another produced a highly accurate and cheap test for pancreatic cancer: http://www.thinkingdigital.co.uk/ speakers/2013/jack-andraka*

- *Australians (and global citizens), including children, can sign a pledge to use the internet for good: http://www. aplatformforgood.org/index.php/pledge/use-your-power-for-good.*
- *There are some great suggestions for summer here, including some fun with technology: http://www.aplatformforgood.org/ summer*

**EXERCISE: Set aside time with your children to think about creative ways of using the net.**

# 3

# Technology: The Toolbox

*There's so much that's positive about technology. The access to information, the ability for our kids to connect with cultures, literature, music and media that opens up their worlds, the education resources, the ability to create media and just the plain fun of gaming – it's all good. The trick is to give our kids the right tools and keep the conversation going.*[1]

Do you need to understand how electricity works in order to turn the light on? No, although knowing how to change a light bulb can help keep them shining. Similarly, you don't need to know everything about how the internet works in order to use it. Increasing your understanding of the most popular tools, however, will help your own confidence, both in using the technology and also in allowing your child to access the right tools.

• • • • • • • • • • • • • • • • • • • • • • • • • • • • • • • • • •

I joined Facebook and made it a condition that I could see their pages, and I insisted on having their computer passwords so I could check their browsing history (I have only had to do so once, and they never did learn to delete it!!). I use the internet a lot myself so I can engage with them

about it. We talk about what we've seen, share
links, etc., so it's part of our conversation, and
we talk about security, user names, ages, etc.

**(Parent, 16 to 18)**

## What's hot right now?

Social media appear to change so fast, with "the latest place
to be" seeming to switch frequently: is it time for us to all
join Google+ now? As with offline hang-outs, however, where
we actually go can remain remarkably stable. The CHILDWISE
Monitor Report of 2013 found that the three favourite sites
for five- to sixteen-year-olds were (in this order) Facebook,
YouTube and Twitter, which have been online since 2004,
2005, and 2006 respectively.[2] We'll look at these sites and a few
others in this section, but note that a Pew Internet survey in
May 2013 revealed that too many adults and too much drama
on Facebook was encouraging teenagers to spend less time on
(not leave) Facebook, meaning they were joining platforms
such as Twitter, Instagram, and Tumblr.[3]

Other sites fall in and out of fashion. In 2010, much of the
concern about teens online centred on Formspring, and in
2013 on Ask.fm, where open questions could be asked, with
sometimes distressing responses, while sites such as Medium,
WhatsApp, Vine, Keek and Pheed are starting to appear in the
"likely to be popular" pile. As mentioned above, take time to
talk to your children about what they're using and ask them to
demonstrate it, and/or keep an eye on the websites suggested at
the end of this book.

## Audio services

There's a range of these online, with the following commonly
mentioned:

**Soundcloud** allows you to upload up to two hours of audio
content online for no fee. Material can then be embedded in

websites and commented on, and users can choose to make a file a "favourite" to return to later.

**Audioboo** uses the web and mobile devices to allow quick, simple, and short recordings when on the move, while adding useful data such as photos, tags, and locations. It can be great for catching people's immediate feedback after events.

**Spotify** is a commercial music streaming service providing rights-protected (a.k.a. legal) content from a range of major and independent record labels. The service had around 20 million users by December 2012, 5 million of them using the paid service, which allows unlimited ad-free listening, including offline.

## Blogging

A blog is an online journal that's updated regularly with entries that appear in reverse chronological order. Blogs can be about any subject, usually something the author is passionate about, and typically contain a mix of text, images, videos, and links to other sites, while encouraging comments from other users. Blogs require a considerable time commitment, but the LSE 2010 study of European children's internet use found that 11 per cent were writing a blog. News stories about nine-year-old Martha's blog "NeverSeconds"[4] have clearly inspired many more children to take up the habit.

Blogger, WordPress, and Tumblr are some of the many (free) blogging platforms available for use. For regular, planned blogging, many find the Blogger site the easiest to use, whereas WordPress has a myriad of extra options and a large user community, and can be hosted under your own domain name. Sites such as Tumblr are particularly popular with the younger generation, being designed to allow for quick and easy posting, scrapbook style.

### What kind of content might I see on my child's blog?

In 2008 Professor David Buckingham looked at a number of personal blog sites produced by children (both boys and girls). The sites were all public, but the content was notably geared to friends. Typical contents included personal pages, declarations of friendship, fan information, and information on their families and cultural heritage, often written in "textspeak", mixed in with coded messages and mobile photos. As children got older, girls in particular became more sarcastic, dropped icons of childhood, developed a more obvious sexuality, and became more critical of adults (especially teachers), while demonstrating an increasing awareness of the world beyond their own websites.[5]

We've emphasized that trust and communication are important, so it's worth considering talking to your child before you read their blog, in case they think you are checking up on them behind their back. This also enables you to open a conversation about the kind of content they have on there, encouraging the good and minimizing the bad. You might want to help them think about what they write, and how, and how it might contribute to their future digital footprint, but don't forget that it's their personal space, in which they may simply want to "play".

### Privacy settings on popular platforms

Most blogs are, by default, set to public viewing, but most can also be set to be read by invited users only.

- **Blogger:** https://support.google.com/blogger/answer/42673?hl=en
- **Tumblr:** http://www.tumblr.com/docs/en/ignoring
- **WordPress:** http://en.support.wordpress.com/settings/privacy-settings/

## Bookmarking

Once, users would store all their "bookmarks" on their own computer, but for years it has been possible to share your links with others online. Sites such as Digg, Delicious, StumbleUpon, and Reddit allow you to submit links, comment on why they've been chosen, and tag with appropriate categories to allow others to find related materials. Teachers are often encouraged to use these tools to collect links for their classes to use. Parents could also use them to create a list of sites that they have vetted for their children to use.

## Facebook

Facebook, created in 2004, was built around a core user base of eighteen- to thirty-four-year-olds, but nowadays users of all age groups can be found on Facebook, with the fastest-growing user group described as grandmothers keen to see pictures of their grandchildren. Facebook famously has over a billion monthly active users worldwide, many of whom use the service to connect with friends they already know offline. Despite stories that people are dropping out of Facebook, overall numbers continue to grow.

• • • • • • • • • • • • • • • • • • • • • • • • • • • • • • • • • • •

Our fourteen-year-old deactivated her Facebook account about a year ago as she had decided it was a waste of her time. I was pleased she had thought this through and was confident enough to go against the crowd. This wasn't down to parental pressure: we both still have FB accounts.
**(Parent, 6 to 9, 10 to 12, 13 to 15)**

Despite the fact that Facebook's Terms of Service limit the site to those over thirteen, the CHILDWISE Monitor Report 2012 found that almost three-quarters of nine- to sixteen-year-olds

48

use Facebook, either with their own account, or through their parents' or friends' accounts. Of these, 33 per cent were classed as active users, with 27 per cent simply passive users: those who have an account and check out what their friends are doing, but rarely post anything.

On Facebook you can send "Friend" requests to other Facebook members, and also receive "Friend" requests, which you can accept, decline, or ignore. You can share updates (including text, photo, and video) on your "Wall", which is on your "Profile" (which can be public or private). Private messages can be shared, instant messaging joined, and photos and check-ins tagged, and users can engage with the pages of celebrities and businesses. You can read a full up-to-date list of Facebook terminology here: https://www.facebook.com/help/219443701509174/

A number of news reports indicate that younger users are continuing to use Facebook, but as a tool because everyone else is there,[6] rather than because it's a site that they are passionate about. Some users find the site too cluttered with posts, "likes", and information from people they agreed to "friend" but don't really know, while it is getting harder to locate the stories that really matter to them.

### *Helpful advice on Facebook*

- https://www.facebook.com/help/ – The Facebook "help" pages are highly functional and full of good advice.
- http://j.mp/WallSTFB – A simple diagrammatic overview of Facebook privacy produced by *The Wall Street Journal*.
- https://www.facebook.com/safety – Pages developed by the Facebook "safety team" for parents, teachers, children, and "law enforcement officers".
- https://www.facebook.com/fbprivacy – A Facebook page that will feed regular practical suggestions into your newsfeed.

### Controlling who sees your stuff

Note that anything your child posts onto a "page" – for example, for a brand they love – is entirely public, but there is more control over personal pages, although always be aware that someone could cut and paste the content.

- Managing who can see and post in your timeline: https://www.facebook.com/help/393920637330807
- Untagging yourself in photos or posts: https://www.facebook.com/help/140906109319589
- Reporting abusive content: https://www.facebook.com/help/181495968648557
- How to block someone from seeing any of your content: https://www.facebook.com/help/168009843260943.

### Deactivating or deleting a Facebook account

Thanks to EU legislation, Facebook's privacy settings for under-eighteens are stronger than for over-eighteens, but if a child lies about their age, then this doesn't help.

- Facebook asks users to report users under thirteen: https://www.facebook.com/help/157793540954833/.
- If any user wants to deactivate (temporarily) or delete (permanently) their account: https://www.facebook. com/help/224562897555674.

## File-hosting service

An internet hosting service specifically designed to host user files, especially large ones that may cause problems if sent by email. These are often uploaded on one device and downloaded on another, sometimes by the same user, often by another user with password access, enabling access to files on the move. Well-known software of this type includes Dropbox, SkyDrive, AVG LiveKive and Google Docs, and they all enable you to access files from anywhere, and save on filling up email inboxes. Software such as Scribd and SlideShare allows for more public sharing of documents.

Be aware that, as data is usually stored on servers distributed around the world, information covered by data protection legislation should not be included in these documents.

## Foursquare

Geolocation-based site Foursquare has 33 million users. Combined with Facebook Places, and a growing number of GPS-enabled smartphones, more and more people are "checking in" to locations, which can then be shared with friends on services such as Facebook and Twitter.

Foursquare allows users to "check in" to tell friends where they are, and track the history of where they've been and whom they've been there with. Users can post photos, comment on each other's posts, and unlock badges, and those who check in to a location more than anyone else can become the "Mayor".

### *Security tips*
- Foursquare recommends that you don't check in to your own home, unless you want to become a potential target for burglary.
- Although the software encourages you to check in regularly, ensure that you are not revealing your regular routine.
- If you are concerned about your privacy, consider checking in as you leave a location, rather than when you arrive.

## Google Search

When we say "search", most of us immediately think of Google. It's worth sounding a note of caution: Google is a commercial company, which filters the content that we can access. Although it remains the default for most web searches, users are increasingly using mobile apps, searching directly on YouTube, or seeking Facebook/Twitter recommendations to find the information they want.

Google can return some interesting responses, and who knows what words your children will be entering (innocently or not)? Accompany them for early searches, have "safe search" turned on to limit any unpleasant surprises, know how to check internet searches, and keep an eye out in case they are just aimlessly searching for hours and could be doing something better with their time.

### Helpful advice for Google Search
- You can turn "safe search" on at http://www.google.co.uk/preferences, ticking the box labelled "Filter explicit results", although it's not foolproof.
- https://www.google.com/insidesearch/tipstricks/all.html gives great advice on the kind of things that you can search for, and how to improve your search results.
- http://www.google.com/trends/hottrends#pn=p9 can provide great conversational starting points, highlighting the current most-searched terms in the UK, while users in other countries can easily select their own country.
- https://support.google.com/accounts/answer/54068?hl=en explains how to check Google's web/search history.

## Google+
Google+ was launched in mid-2011, and has been described by Google as a "social layer" that enhances many of its online properties, and therefore differs from a conventional social network. In mid-2012 it allowed users over thirteen to join up. Many dismiss it as a space occupied only by tumbleweed, but it had 359 million monthly active users as of May 2013, and "+1" (similar to a Facebook "Like") affects Google Search results.

*Helpful advice on Google+*
- http://www.google.com/intl/en/+/safety/ is designed for teens, parents, and educators and gives details of particular safety features that have been designed for under-eighteens.

## Instagram

Instagram (now owned by Facebook) has 100 million users. It's an online photo-sharing service that encourages its users to take pictures, apply digital filters to photos (change how they look), and share them on other social networking services. The software says that users should be over thirteen, although there are no checks in place.

A 2013 survey by Pew Internet found that teenagers rated Instagram as the third most popular social network (despite not being in the list provided).[7] Teens indicated that they liked the simplicity of the app, enjoyed it, and found that there weren't too many adults on it. With cameras on most mobile phones, and the many celebrities who have profiles on the app, its popularity is not surprising.

For those who are concerned to fully own the rights to their own photos, "Pressgram" http://pressgr.am was launched in September 2013.

*What does a parent need to know about Instagram?*
- Connectsafely.org have written a beautifully simple guide for parents. Download it at: http://www.connectsafely.org/wp-content/uploads/instagram_guide.pdf.

## LinkedIn

LinkedIn has the strongest reputation in the business world, and is useful to build content on, particularly if you're looking for work in the corporate world, as it's the first "social media site" that many managers are prepared to join.

LinkedIn has over 200 million users, who can import their CVs, connect with known professional contacts, and demonstrate their expertise. It is particularly good for headhunters, job hunters and entrepreneurs.

## Pinterest

Launched in 2010, but taking off in popularity in January 2012, Pinterest is an image-based bookmarking site, with 48.7 million users as of May 2013. Users can collect material on themed "boards", as if pinning it to a pinboard. The images "pinned" link back to the source page that the image was taken from (it's recommended that you don't upload images unless they are your own), and other users can share images. Some statistics say that users spend as long on Pinterest as they do on Facebook, as they share inspirational ideas, quotes, infographics, and things that they want to buy.

The software is very simple to use, but help is provided here: https://help.pinterest.com/home, including how to block or report users for inappropriate images.

## Snapchat

Snapchat is a photo-messaging application for mobile phones, recommended for those aged twelve and over, but particularly popular with those aged thirteen to twenty-four. The app is very simple to use for sharing pictures and video clips (accompanied by doodles and text if desired) with friends and family. Images can be shared for only up to ten seconds and then the content "disappears", and every day more than 50 millions Snapchat messages are shared worldwide.

The fact that the image "disappears" gives the illusion of control, but it's still possible for the recipient to capture a screenshot of the image (although if the receiver's phone device is used for this, you'll be sent an alert), and the information will have passed through computer servers, where copies may continue to exist.

## What does a parent need to know about Snapchat?

- Connectsafely.org have written a very simple guide for parents. Download it at: http://www.connectsafely.org/wp-content/uploads/snapchat_guide.pdf.

## Skype

Skype (now owned by Microsoft) allows instant messaging, file transfer, and video conferencing. Calls to other users of the service are free, while calls to other landlines and mobile phones can be made for a fee. Chats can be copied and stored elsewhere, although there's no inbuilt ability to save conversations, but purchasing software such as Pamela for Skype can allow recordings.

Skype is designed for those over thirteen, and the service encourages "parents to be involved in the online activities of their children to make sure that no information is collected from a child without parental permission".

### What about younger users?

A service known as Skypito has been designed with Skype for users aged two to fourteen: http://www.skypito.com/, with a simpler interface, and in which all potential contacts have to be approved by parents.

## Twitter

Twitter, created in 2006, is a form of microblogging, initially based on text messages. "Tweets" are limited to 140 characters, displayed, and delivered to the author's "followers". A "retweet" (RT) occurs when another user reposts your message, thus circulating it to their followers – a true compliment. Twitter is great for making and maintaining contacts with others with similar interests, with hashtags, e.g. #digitalparenting, used within tweets, functioning as active links.

In May 2013 the site had over 500 million registered accounts, of which 288 million were active monthly users, with particular growth among fifty-five- to sixty-four-year-olds. Recent surveys by Common Sense Media (USA) and the CHILDWISE Monitor Report 2012 (UK) indicate that around 25 per cent of teenagers now use Twitter, with fifteen- to sixteen-year-old girls in the UK tweeting most regularly, and an increasing number reading others' tweets. Other factors driving teenagers (under-thirteens shouldn't be on it) towards Twitter will be that celebrities are using it, newsreaders and TV programmes advertise Twitter user names and hashtags, and an increasing number of their friends are on the site.

### Helpful advice on Twitter
- https://support.twitter.com/groups/57-safety-security gives clear advice on how to adapt your settings and tweet responsibly, with tips for teens, parents, and schools, as well as what to do if you see suicidal and self-harm-related content on Twitter.

## YouTube
YouTube (now owned by Google) was created in 2005. It is a video-sharing website on which users can upload and share videos, and create themed playlists of favourite saved videos. In January 2012 YouTube said that sixty hours of new videos were uploaded to the site every minute. In May 2013 the site had 1 billion unique monthly visitors, with a particularly active eighteen to thirty-four age group, with around 6 billion hours of videos watched every month.

As are many other sites, YouTube is designed for over-thirteens, but there's plenty of material for younger children to watch with their parents (I've seen my fair share of Elmo, The Wheels on the Bus and Peppa Pig, among others). Children interviewed for the CHILDWISE Media Report 2012 showed that the most active users were boys (with 18 per cent having an account, although the majority watch YouTube without an account).

As one eleven- to thirteen-year-old said: "You can find anything on there." YouTube is now the second most popular search engine, and is particularly useful for "how-to" videos – learn how to play the guitar or fix the car – but do watch out for the quality of the information.

There *is* a lot of great information on YouTube, but also a lot of inappropriate content. YouTube has a safety mode (turn it on or off at the base of your YouTube page), but YouTube itself admits that it's not particularly effective, and a quick search for "YouTube safety mode" will bring up multiple videos instructing users how to turn it off!

### Helpful advice on YouTube

There's a good range of information on http://www.youtube.com/yt/policyandsafety/safety.html. Specific items you may be interested in include:

- Creating and editing playlists, particularly for younger children: http://support.google.com/youtube/bin/answer.py?hl=en-GB&answer=57792
- Making a video private, to be shared with only fifty users: http://support.google.com/youtube/bin/answer.py?hl=en-GB&answer=157177

Be aware that comments on YouTube are not always the most edifying, so advance approval can be set for comments before they are posted – and it may be worth your screening comments, especially if your child has uploaded something creative: http://support.google.com/youtube/bin/answer.py?hl=en-GB&answer=58123

### Dealing with offensive videos

Owing to the sheer scale of YouTube uploads, the approach to offensive videos has to be reactive rather than proactive. This does mean that if a video you wish you hadn't uploaded attracts unwanted interest, although it can be deleted there is time for copies to be made, so think before uploading.

YouTube actively works to remove inappropriate material, including sexting, malicious pranks, mocking parodies, and violent fights, but it can take several hours, again because of the amount of data. If you find a video that infringes community guidelines, look at http://www.youtube.com/t/community_guidelines: there's a "Flag" button next to each video http://support.google.com/youtube/bin/answer.py?hl=en&answer=2802027&rd=1

## Don't forget the "old" technologies

It may be easy to keep in touch with your children online via the "Send" button, but if you're out and about, postcards and phone calls are still much appreciated by many. We'll return later in the book to the strategies that some parents use to ensure that all technologies are part of a wider range of choices that their children can access.

> **EXERCISE: Look through the list and/or talk to your child about which tools they are using, and pick one to focus on for a couple of weeks to improve your knowledge of and confidence with it.**

# 4

# Children in Digital Culture

In the early days online, internet usage at school was an initial driver in getting many children involved, but with near-universal access at home the internet is now seen as being primarily for leisure activities. Many children wouldn't really describe anything that they do at school as "using the internet", as it is generally so locked down that they are unable to access many sites. In this chapter we want to start to understand the digital culture that children are engaging with. What is positive, and what is negative?

Reports in recent years have given us an idea of how many children spend time online, how much time they spend, and what they do there. The EU Kids Online Project, run by the LSE, found that a significant number of under-thirteens have online profiles, even though most social networks, such as Facebook, require members to be at least thirteen years old. A growing number are accessing the online world via mobile devices.[1] The latest payment packages for broadband and mobile phones have removed constraints that previously held back access, and laptops, tablets, and e-readers have reached a price at which they are attractive as presents. (See the UK Office of Communications (Ofcom) "Children and Parents: Media Use and Attitudes Report" (2012) for some of the latest in-depth statistics for children's use of new media.[2])

The CHILDWISE Monitor Report 2012 highlighted that the most common activities for primary school children online are playing games and watching video clips, while those over eleven are more likely to be engaging in communications activities, such as social networking or instant messaging. We need to educate our children to use technology in a balanced way: misbehaviour hasn't changed as much as the ways of carrying it out. In order to give children clear, definable boundaries and some structure online, learn about the spaces that they are engaging with but, more importantly, understand the different ways that they engage with them. In 2010, the BBC provided a quiz that offered insights into the range of behaviours online,[3] while a group at Massachusetts Institute of Technology (MIT) offer a deeper insight into understanding introverted and extroverted behaviour, and the importance of starting with the people using the technology rather than the technology itself.[4]

## The myth of "the digital native"

The CHILDWISE "Digital Lives" Report of 2010 proudly noted: "Today's young children are born into a digital world, and have never known a time without the internet affecting all aspects of their daily life." That may be true, but it tends to be translated into a kind of panic:

. . . . . . . . . . . . . . . . . . . . . . . . . . . . . . .

It's a minefield!! It has been a tricky path to stay one step ahead in an area [technology] that has developed so much, as we have become parents and never navigated it before ourselves [as children].
**(Parent, 19 or over)**

We need to appreciate, however, that using technology doesn't mean that we understand how it works, any more than driving a car means that we are mechanics. Terms have been coined such as "digital natives" or "net generation", which all perpetuate this idea that every child knows what they are doing online. Parents seem to agree:

. . . . . . . . . . . . . . . . . . . . . . . . . . . . . . . . . . . . .

The children usually know more than we do, and I think that is one of the problems. Computers didn't exist when I was at school, so I didn't learn anything about them; I've had to learn everything as an adult, and probably sometimes I've been a few steps behind my children!

**(Parent, 16 to 18, 19 or over)**

. . . . . . . . . . . . . . . . . . . . . . . . . . . . . . . . . . . . .

It feels like a minefield as I step into this stage of parenting and realize that I will most likely be a step behind my digitally native children! However, with guidelines in place, I believe that digital tools offer children a unique learning opportunity and are of general benefit to family life.

**(Parent, 2 or under, 3 to 5)**

If we buy into the idea that children are "digital natives", who are fundamentally different from "the rest of us", we can cause serious confidence problems for parents. Traits such as collaboration, innovation, transparency, and openness are often ascribed to the younger generation, and they may indeed be found there, but research demonstrates that they can also be observed across all generations. The EU Kids Online study in 2012 found that only about 20 per cent of the 25,000 children they interviewed fitted this stereotype.[5] I have observed many students who are entirely happy using social networks such as Facebook, but struggle to conduct effective online searches, something that has been evidenced by others at e-learning conferences. Every generation is different, but there are factors other than technology that may account for the differences.

Marc Prensky popularized the term "digital native" in 2001, referring to those in the US education system who had grown up surrounded by technology. A more useful idea has developed from a team at Oxford University led by Dave White: that of the "digital resident" and the "digital visitor", defined more by attitude than by age. "Visitors" use the internet as a tool: go in to complete a task, and leave. "Residents" regard themselves as members of communities that exist online, rather than having access to an online toolbox.[6] I am most definitely a digital resident, though I'm far too old to be a "digital native".

## Children online

For all of us, the online environment has changed. We increasingly have wireless broadband at home, we have more mobile devices, it's easy to segue between online and offline, we have more control over the things we watch via time-shifted TV, we are able to shop online, search for information online, store material "in the cloud", keep connected with people even when we've moved on through social networks, and use GPS for a range of functions. The rate of change means that there *are* major differences in experience across age groups – those who can remember a time before broadband, before smartphones, before Facebook, before the Nintendo Wii – and we read our experiences differently according to what we've experienced before.

In the past, the adults in their lives would have introduced children to the world slowly: family and local neighbours, then national, then international. With the internet, there truly is a global world at our fingertips from the get-go – and there's no point saying "You can't have", as most children will just find access at someone else's house. The reality that the CHILDWISE reports have demonstrated is that older children are using the internet to talk with friends whom they already see every day, continuing the conversation, sharing notes, and making plans.

Younger children focus more on keeping in touch with friends and family members who live further away:

```
Facebook... is a brilliant tool for communicating
messages to dispersed groups of people and for
maintaining contact with friends and loved ones, and
allowing a more intimate involvement in family lives,
e.g. grandparents sharing their grandchildren growing
up, even if they live far away.
```
**(Parent, 16 to 18)**

```
I like the fact that communication is so instant.
They can talk to their uncle/aunt/cousins (my
brother in Australia) over Skype. I think I know
more about their life because of Facebook than my
parents knew of mine!
```
**(Parent, 16 to 18, 19 or over)**

### Making positive choices
Increased time spent online *will* most likely increase exposure to negative experiences – but also the positive opportunities. Nancy Willard, a cyberbullying expert, calls for us to work on the "understanding that the vast majority of young people want to make good choices, do not want to be harmed, and do not want to see their friends or others harmed".[7] We can't control their whole environment, online or offline, so parents need to give their children the capability to deal with problems as they come across them.

Dr Leslie Haddon, who was involved in the LSE EU Kids Online study of 25,000 children in Europe, said:

*Children are not all the same... much of what is considered risky by one child will be considered not problematic by others. So, the most important recommendation is to ask*

*children what bothers them online, listen to what they have
to say and help them accordingly.*[8]

*The CHILDWISE "Digital Lives" Report asked children to go back in time
and explain to Victorian children what the internet was.*

Many of the oldest tried to explain *how the internet works*, but
others, and especially the younger children, focused on *what
the internet enables them to do* – a place to communicate, to
find things out, to play games, to create and have fun. Several
referred explicitly to the all-encompassing nature of what is on
offer to them via the internet. (My italics.)

**EXERCISE: Get your child to choose their audience – a child
from the past, an alien, someone from a deep jungle – and
try to explain the internet to them. Discuss any insights
that emerge from the discussions.**

## What changes in the teenage years?

When young people reach thirteen, their online options
expand hugely. US law, which affects most social networks,
restricts legal access to sites such as Facebook, Twitter, and
Snapchat, although many children are online before this
age – often with their parents' blessing (we'll return to that).
As an accessible group with high potential spending power
from pocket money or part-time earnings, and one that has
high ownership of technological devices, this group has been
researched significantly. A Pew Internet survey in 2010 ranked
the seven main ways that seventeen-year-olds communicated.
In descending order:
- text messaging
- cell/mobile phone calls
- landline calls
- face to face

- social networks
- instant messaging
- email.

Written letters did not even merit a footnote. Pew discovered that teenage girls averaged around eighty texts a day and boys around thirty,[9] with Nielsen totalling this at over 3,000 per month (or six per waking hour).[10]

Jeff Jarvis, a journalist from the US/UK, spoke thus of his fifteen-year-old:

*Jake told the executive that he never goes directly to a brand like this man's newspaper or even to blogs he likes… he reads a lot of news – far more than I did at his age. But he goes to that news only via the links from Digg, friends' blogs, and Twitter. He travels all around the Internet that is edited by his peers because he trusts them and knows they share his interests. The web of trust is built at eye level, peer-to-peer.[11]*

This gives a sense that this is unique to teenagers, but most of us will choose what we buy based on the experiences and recommendations of those we trust.

As we have noted, online and offline are part of the same whole, and many would say that it is a normal part of adolescence to test boundaries, challenge adult norms, experiment with relationships, play with identities, explore new sexual experiences, keep or break secrets, exclude or be excluded by peers, deceive parents, and worry about one's development. All this is to be expected online as it is offline, but online things can spread faster and be manipulated or shared in more unexpected ways.[12] The emotional and developmental state of teenagers is referred to by many researchers, who warn against posting material while upset, as this can cause longer-term damage (a piece of advice that would be good for adults to take on board too!).

If you want to read a well-researched but highly readable recent account, check out Chris Davies and Rebecca Eynon's *Teenagers and Technology* (2013), which surveyed the experiences of 1,000 children, 200 of them in-depth. The book seeks to show that teenagers have very variable experiences with technology, from those who love it to those who are ambivalent or negative about it. Habits formed in teenage years tend to remain with us throughout our studies and working lives, and parents feel the pressure of ensuring that their children are able to "keep up" through technology. The authors consider the typical experience of teenagers in the Western world, and "do not buy the notion that young people, teenagers especially, are going somewhere that is beyond the understanding of the rest of us by virtue of their access to technologies".[13]

Davies and Eynon do emphasize that parental attitudes are vital, whether resistant to, or supportive of, technologies. If you're one of those parents who don't hover over your children online, you are not alone. Such parents tend not to vocalize such a lack of concern because it suggests a laissez-faire attitude to children's safety that is not seen as OK in today's risk-managed world. The authors also highlight the particular difficulties of separated families, where parents may have completely different attitudes to internet usage, which children have to learn to negotiate. They note that younger teenagers, excited to be finally allowed onto Facebook, find it "a necessary addition to their social lives, but not so much fun as they had expected".[14]

The teenage years are typically seen as those of identity formation: "… teenagers are trying to grow up, relying less on parents, making stronger relationships with peers, and trying to make choices about their future."[15] Many learn the "social norms" by observing what others are doing on their profiles (a.k.a. "lurking"), so that they can present themselves in a good light, and determine who "deserves" a quick reply. Most are aware of their audience (including parents and future employers), and seek to be authentic, but that authenticity is determined by context. For those starting university, where a Facebook page is provided for new starters, casual comments can develop into deeper conversations and into friendships that can last through university.

For many teenagers, technology has become naturalized into daily life, and is no longer noticeable as technology – many are not interested in something *because* it's technological, but in what it can do for them. Teenagers tend to use their tech more in the evenings, staying within the protection of the home while gaining freedom, saving their weekends as a chance to get out of the house. Davies and Eynon note that the online world provides a safe space for, for example, sexual exploration of minority groups (conversations which can then be studied – after obtaining user permission – because all digital data is recorded, offering insights that can affect future policy decisions).[16] Several commentators have noted that digital technology has given teenagers (in particular) extra freedom, but the ownership of devices is often economically dependent upon their parents, which is at odds with actual autonomy.

## Buy me! Buy me!

*Parents do say no. They say no, you can't stay up late. No, you can't eat pudding before your main course. No, you can't have a dog. Setting boundaries is what parents do. It's tough sometimes… and I need to ask if the advertising industry is comfortable spending millions of pounds targeting children direct and then saying it's down to Mum and Dad to stand up to them.*

**(Parent, quoted in the Bailey Review, 2011)**

Children are involved in making buying decisions from a very early age, but concern over the amount of advertising they are exposed to online was raised in the Bailey Review "Letting Children Be Children: The Report of an Independent Review of the Commercialisation and Sexualisation of Childhood" (2011).[17] Online advertising has grown significantly in recent years with sites such as Club Penguin, owned by Disney and typically promoting their latest film. This online/offline crossover is noticeable with most brands – wherever they start, they end up in the other space, with many opportunities to "invest" in merchandise.

Advertising is becoming increasingly personalized. As I write this, I am being followed around the internet by some of the bathroom suites I have been researching for my house. We mostly seem to accept that we get entertainment and websites at the cost of advertising. In the CHILDWISE Monitor Report 2012, parents expressed particular concerns about adverts sent to mobile phones, and said they had been significantly "pestered" into purchasing something. Although many children find online ads annoying or distracting, a significant number don't even notice them, and 20 per cent would never click on them. A further 15 per cent said they found it hard sometimes to work out what was an advert, and 11 per cent had noticed that adverts were for things of particular interest to them, or understood that the adverts were the price they paid for "free services". There's no such thing as a free lunch, and without advertising most of these sites wouldn't exist. We have got used to this through systems such as Tesco Clubcard points. Google "targeted advertising" if you want to understand how this works, and you'll probably pick up a range of tips for filtering some adverts out.

We live in a world that is defined by "pull" marketing rather than "push" marketing. With "push" marketing, you continually broadcast a message in the hope that someone will give in. Most social media, however, and the advertising within them, focus on "pull" marketing, where we "opt in" to receive newsletters, personalized ads, blog feeds, and coupons in return for our data, because something has attracted our interest. Note also that "Liking", "Retweeting" or "G+" are all part of the "social circle" of advertising: all your connections can potentially see what you've liked, and are then more likely to like it for themselves. Be wary, however, of adverts that offer to give you "free iPads" and the like: they are likely to be pages simply seeking to build up a significant number of "Likes", so that they can sell "popular" pages.[18]

The internet allows pre-purchase investigations, price comparisons, in-purchase decisions, and post-purchase instructions. As digital research company eMarketer notes on the Vodafone website:

> *In making purchase decisions, teens rely on social media and mobile phones in both conventional and innovative ways. They share news about bargains with close friends via text messaging; they use the built-in camera on their phones to snap photos while trying on clothes, then upload the pictures to Facebook.[19]*

Most money in the online economy is spent not *by* young people but *on* them by parents, often working together with their children to make decisions. Parents need to be aware of the huge pressures placed on youth in particular to feel "cool", and the constant barrage of sexualized images of teens, and seek to focus on areas other than appearance in discussions about spending money.

Anything that requires payment is always an issue, as children have limited spending power, and if an alternative activity has to be sacrificed it's likely they won't pay for downloads. Many children rely on their parents for funding, and then don't consider the cost at all. A number of parents, wanting their children to have a better grasp of the value of money, have looked for solutions to ad hoc payouts. These have included a fixed budget for apps, a nominal cost per minute for internet access (e.g. 1p), or setting a pay rate for particular jobs. Children can compete for these, and the rate of pay will fall if the jobs are not completed within a specified time frame. Payments are then made into the child's PayPal account.[20]

Martin Lewis's Money Saving Expert site gives some advice on the importance of pocket money,[21] and he has campaigned successfully for financial education in schools.[22] If you want an electronic solution, look for software such as VirtualPiggy, A+Allowance, or iAllowance.

> **EXERCISE: Take a look at how you handle money with your children. What pocket money practices do you have? What might you need to alter?**

## "Digital divide"

Computers have been sold to parents on the basis that they are essential for their children's education, whereas children are marketed to on the basis of "fun and games" (not that the two have to be mutually exclusive!). Most parents now agree that computers are necessary across the board, but in all this we appear to be working on the assumption that children have access to digital devices, and that parents can afford pocket money.

• • • • • • • • • • • • • • • • • • • • • • • • • • • • • • • • • • • •

We believe that modern tech needs to be more available and cheaper, including free Wi-Fi or broadband for those underprivileged families or those on benefits, to enable parents to engage with their children on these matters.

**(Parent, 13 to 15)**

We live in a society in which technology, rather than just being something we use, is embedded in most people's lives, so what happens to those who don't have good access to it? This is known as the "digital divide", and is rather beyond the scope of this book. If your family is one of the 10 per cent that don't have a computer at home, it is worth making your child's teachers aware that their online activities will have to be restricted to homework tasks. There will be few opportunities to experiment and play, as such homework has to be done within a tight time frame, at school or in the public library.[23]

Schools may have computing equipment, but the attitude of the teachers who manage it can make a significant difference to the experience that children have with it. This is also true of those at home: research indicates that parents who are better educated in the use of digital technology (as this book is aiming to help you be) give more proactive support to their children online, whereas those without this confidence tend to set regulations and use technical means to limit access. The 2010 CHILDWISE "Digital Lives" Report raises the often-forgotten factor of unreliable or broken equipment, which has a big impact on "true Internet accessibility".

## Where do children turn for advice?

Professor Sonia Livingstone and her team conducted research across Europe for EU Kids Online, and were surprised to find that parents still have such a strong role in advising, setting rules, and supporting children online, particularly when they encounter risks there. As children get older, they are more likely to turn to their friends, who may have been the catalyst for their wanting to go online in the first place. Research has demonstrated that at present most parental involvement is triggered only by a negative experience, so we need to be more proactive in helping children engage online.[24]

Research has also shown that a significant majority of children do not report negative online experiences, either because they are afraid their parents will overreact, or because they feel they are able to take responsibility and fix the problem themselves (or feel they should be able to do so). A belief in their ability to handle difficult situations effectively on their own is an important life skill for teenagers to acquire.

**EXERCISE: Take time to think whom your child talks to, and how you can help encourage/build on those conversations.**

• • • • • • • • • • • • • • • • • • • • • • • • • • • • • • • • • •

Discussion has proved the best way for us to control the use of digital tech, combined with rules for the amount of usage. The most important thing for us has been to keep discussion going so that our sons don't feel they have to hide what they're doing from us.

**(Parent, 13 to 15, 16 to 18)**

The more trustworthy people children have to confide in, the less likely it is that they will turn to strangers for advice. So, how do parents ensure that they come to them for the support required? It is all down to communication...

# 5

# Communicate, Communicate, Communicate

· · · · · · · · · · · · · · · · · · · · · · · · · · · · · · · · · ·

We trust them, and our open, ongoing conversation
with them about these matters means that they
quickly inform us of anything that worries them [and
we] believe that [this] is the key to prevention,
not enforcement.

**(Parent, 13 to 15)**

At the heart of the advice I give, and what every book on this
subject states, is that appropriate adults need to talk to children
about their online activities and behaviour, providing space to
listen and discuss any issues that arise. *This is the most powerful
and effective weapon you have in your parenting toolbox.* The digital
world is part of children's lives: it's here to stay, and there are
plenty of opportunities available online, so let's help children
make the most of it – safely, in among all the other activities
that fill their lives!

We openly discuss what is appropriate and why, without going into too much detail. It is about building trust now, so when he is older he can be trusted to use things sensibly when not under our watchful eyes.

**(Parent, 6 to 9)**

Reg Bailey, Chief Executive of the Mothers' Union, undertook a review for the government on the "Commercialisation and Sexualisation of Childhood" in 2011. This indicated that parents approach talking to their children about technology in similar ways to talking about sex. They are nervous about where the conversation will go and not quite sure where to start, and equally unsure how to sell the positives without focusing too much on the negatives. Tim Woda, co-founder of uKnowKids, encourages us not to think of these as technology problems, but as parenting problems:[1]

*Set the boundaries, set the expectations. It's your child's job to adhere to those expectations. It is your job to be in tune enough to understand when it is time to expand their independent use of technology. It is not your child's role to define your role in their digital life.[2]*

In many parenting books, you will find reference to Dr Diana Baumrind, who defined four basic parenting styles:
1. Authoritative: actively involved in a positive manner
2. Authoritarian: actively involved but in a negative manner
3. Indulgent: positively involved but not active
4. Neglectful: negatively involved and not active.

As you may expect from those definitions, she encourages authoritative parenting, in which rules and limits are set in discussion with the child, and the child is encouraged to be open about hopes, fears, and worries. This approach has been proved to encourage positive engagement online.

In the same way as you're beside your child when they learn to crawl, walk, and ride a bike, right up to when they learn to drive, you have to teach them to respect the digital environment, look for the opportunities, and be aware of the potential dangers. Talk to them about what they are seeing and experiencing, give them freedom within boundaries as you would in any other space, get to know whom they are friends with online, discuss costs and timing (and not just when these become a problem), define consequences, and consider particular scenarios and get them to think about how they might react. It is not helpful to monitor children without letting them know that you are doing so, otherwise you may lose their trust. Just let your children know that the only reason you're keeping an eye on them is to help them if they get into difficulties, and teach them to respect, not fear, what technology can do. A parenting website in the UK says:

*As digital technology plays an increasingly important role in our lives, core parenting skills are still important. Giving a child a sense of belonging, teaching them about interdependence as well as independence, and having the confidence to offer a sense of meaning to their lives remain crucial.*[3]

• • • • • • • • • • • • • • • • • • • • • • • • • • • • • • • •

I never challenge her about things I observe directly, but use the information to begin a dialogue, and very gently let her know that I'm aware. She is nearly sixteen, and as a result of guiding her over the last few years I feel she is learning how to manage herself well online. She's certainly observed some out-of-control horror stories with her friends, which has been a sharp learning exercise! It also simply means that I can always get in touch with her, and she has the freedom to be out and about but remain connected.

**(Parent, 13 to 15)**

*A couple of books that may help you talk to your child:*
- *Alastair Somerville, "Isabel Online: Just a story about being a young person, online" (2013) about "life online"*
- *"Digiduck's big decision" (re cyberbullying): http://kidsmart.org.uk/teachers/ks1/digiduck.aspx*

*Where do some of the questionnaire respondents get their information on best practice from?*

• • • • • • • • • • • • • • • • • • • • • • • • • • • • • •

Active user myself, so I am as up to date as possible, and basic security measures. Reading up on social networking for teens (not at that stage yet) and asking advice of parents with older kids.

**(Parent, 2 or under, 3 to 5, 6 to 9)**

• • • • • • • • • • • • • • • • • • • • • • • • • • • • • •

So far the most effective method has been discussions about what is appropriate for them to be doing, and discussing the pitfalls and folly of what some of their friends are already doing.

**(Parent, 10 to 12)**

• • • • • • • • • • • • • • • • • • • • • • • • • • • • • •

Would be good to attend a meeting where parents can share solutions about concerns and receive advice, e.g. at local school.

**(Parent, 10 to 12)**

Take the time to open up discussions with other parents, whether at the school gates or on sites such as Mumsnet. Be free with your expertise, and don't be afraid to ask "stupid questions". As those who really need this kind of book probably won't be reading it, encourage your children to pass on the good practices you have instilled in them to those whose parents can't or won't do so. It's helpful in these situations to have older students give insights into their life, offer resources in school, and add brief tips to student newsletters in order to share their expertise with the community. *In every interaction with your child in relation to digital technologies, ensure there is at least one positive statement about your child's activities.* This is known as "operant conditioning" – it means your child will be more likely to want to share aspects of their digital life with you.

. . . . . . . . . . . . . . . . . . . . . . . . . . . . . . . . . . . .

> We sit down periodically, particularly after a new service emerges, and discuss their possible access to and use of it. We don't spy on them daily, but do occasionally sit alongside them while they are online and discuss what they are doing. In the main this is while helping them with homework and projects, but we trust them, and we believe that trust and constant, ongoing conversation are the keys to prevention, not enforcement.
>
> **(Parent, 13 to 15)**

Regarding creating a space for these discussions, Chelsea Clinton (daughter of ex-US President Bill Clinton) has recalled how media had their place in her household as she grew up. Neither the television nor the radio was on during meals, and media consumption was a family experience. Media (of all sorts) in and surrounding their lives were a frequent conversational topic, designed to encourage a "healthy scepticism" for the bad times, as well as an honest and open relationship in the good ones.[4]

So, how often are you going to have a conversation about the media that your family are using? Beth Blecherman, founder of TechMamas.com, has a daily talk with her children about the sites they are using, offering a space to catch "problems" before they get too far out of hand.[5] I'd suggest you think about a short, weekly session, either round the dinner table or with all sitting at the same eye level. Decide whether you will turn the technology off, or make it an active part of the conversation. Think about the kinds of topic you would like to discuss, such as:

- What have you seen this week, and what did you enjoy?
- What's the most exciting thing you learned this week?
- Have you ever seen images online that made you feel uncomfortable? How did you feel when you saw them?

You will develop further ideas of questions as you work through this, but your role in these conversations is to introduce important topics, then sit and listen carefully, without judgment, to ensure that your child will want to talk to you.

### The question of an Internet Safety Agreement

*What do some of the questionnaire respondents think about implementing an Internet Safety Agreement?*

● ● ● ● ● ● ● ● ● ● ● ● ● ● ● ● ● ● ● ● ● ● ● ● ● ● ● ● ● ● ● ● ● ● ● ●

I'm surprised at how many parents seem to be "hands off" with rules, settings, etc. when they are so careful about ferrying children to school safely, etc. When I talk about it with parents of younger children, the response is "They know more about it than I do" — but that doesn't make much sense when the parents are in their twenties and should be savvy themselves. It's almost become a motto!

**(Aunt/Uncle, 10 to 12)**

Most books and websites dealing with this topic will recommend a "Family Internet Agreement". Some offer simple agreements for the family to sign, but research demonstrates that families should discuss specifically with their children what should be in such an agreement, and for which ages, and create something that fits in with the family's values, such as a three-column sheet with "Yes, we can", "Don't like it", and "Don't even think about it", with the rules potentially moving columns as the children get older.

It's worth taking time to agree what the consequences should be for breaking the rules. Boundaries will be pushed, and rules will be broken. As an example, if your child is found texting at 3 a.m., keep the device in your room overnight for a month, returning it each morning, with stricter punishments for repeated rule breaking. In the most effective agreements, parents also agree what their own internet practices will be.

The CHILDWISE "Digital Lives" Report 2010 noted that many parents had such agreements in place (only about a fifth didn't), but took compliance largely on trust, and that a desire to avoid confrontation meant messages weren't enforced. Carrie Longton from Mumsnet noted:

> To be honest, I'm not sure we've stuck to everything… But it opened a dialogue. It made us sit down and think as a family what we all wanted from technology. It didn't make us all agree, but it helped us see where we didn't.[6]

Parents should concentrate on developing positive behaviour in children, rather than focusing only on undesirable behaviour. With regard to an Internet Safety Agreement, ensure that your children realize that you simply want to understand the spaces they are in, to encourage them to be responsible and help them understand that there's good material online. Children need to grasp that everyone is being watched, all net activity leaves "digital fingerprints", and there are legal ramifications of net abuse.

**EXERCISE: Start to think about what will be included in your family Internet Safety Agreement, which you can develop further as you work through this book.**

. . . . . . . . . . . . . . . . . . . . . . . . . . . . . . . . . . . .

With such young kids we have yet to establish any set rules, although we should probably start thinking about that. So far we only allow use when one of us is helping.
**(Parent, 2 or under, 3 to 5)**

As you read through the next section, you will gain an understanding of the areas that are relevant to your family, and be able to configure your own family internet agreement, and truly understand how to enjoy the best, and avoid the worst, of what is online.

# 6

# Practical Advice for Parents in a Digital Age

Ofcom's 2012 survey found that managing the day-to-day impact of the internet on family life, such as the need to create family time away from the computer, to enforce bedtimes or to encourage physical activity, was of more immediate concern to parents than the risks of grooming, cyberbullying or access to inappropriate content.[1] This section looks at some of the practical steps you can take to give your children the best experience online, not forgetting the simple advice given in a 2009 UK government campaign: "Zip It, Block It, Flag It".[2]

Martha Payne, the nine-year-old food blogger of "NeverSeconds",[3] gave (with a little help from Mum and Dad) a series of tips on how her family have found ways to embed the digital into their lives. These included time limits (they have a budget of one hour each per day), the computer remains in public spaces, Dad has the passwords to the blog and sees any comments first, facts should be questioned, no form filling without Mum or Dad, and she clicks to minimize the window if there's anything she doesn't like. Mostly, she says, remember to have fun. In the process of writing this blog, she raised large sums of money for Mary's Meals.[4]

## Appropriate at what age?

Martha's family had clearly taken the time to think about what was appropriate for a nine-year-old. Each age will come with different challenges, but as one questionnaire respondent said:

- - - - - - - - - - - - - - - - - - - - - - - - - - - - - - - - - - - - -

You need to look at each individual, not necessarily the age.

**(Parent, 6 to 9)**

Many providers of advice have moved away from age-defined categories, possibly because Professor Tanya Byron emphasized in 2008 that we need to focus on the individual strengths and vulnerabilities of each child. The factors that define "beneficial" and "harmful" experiences online and in video games will vary according to each child and their personal development. Another respondent to the questionnaire wrote:

- - - - - - - - - - - - - - - - - - - - - - - - - - - - - - - - - - - - -

Age restriction is more about their ability not to lose expensive gadgets than about access to inappropriate material.

**(Parent, 13 to 15)**

Most age-related material correlates with school years, but the emphasis is on knowing your own child, rather than caring about national averages:

- - - - - - - - - - - - - - - - - - - - - - - - - - - - - - - - - - - - -

We have always been strict about not allowing our children to own age-inappropriate films and games, and have operated a "buy-back policy" for games and music that our children have bought but about whose content we feel unhappy, even if it has been "legal". (We have given them back the money these things cost so they can get something more suitable, and then disposed of the offending media, or kept them till they were older.) Of course that has not stopped our children from seeing things at school or friends' houses, but we have attempted to be open about our reasons for the age-restriction ban, and all three of our children seem to have abided by our decisions.

**(Parent, 16 to 18, 19 or over)**

The expectation is that, as you would in any other space, you will create a "walled garden" for your children when very young, allowing them to use only the websites that you have identified and bookmarked, relaxing this as they get older, and replacing supervision with discussion.

Professor Byron gave extensive insights into the developmental stages of children in the 2008 report, which I have attempted to summarize here.

**Pre-school:** Children's lives are focused strongly on family and the home, especially on developing relationships with the key adults in their lives. At this age children have little ability to differentiate between reality and fantasy, so find violence and emotional scenes hard to handle. Their "online diet" needs to be supervised and restricted in respect of both content and time.

**Five to eleven years:** As children start school, they begin to develop relationships with more people outside the family, including learning the social norms of friendships with other children, learning right and wrong, and distinguishing reality from fantasy. At this age parents need to allow greater freedoms, but still within boundaries and accompanied by more discussion: "This enables the child to develop their own critical evaluation and self-management skills as well as being supported when they cannot or, as in the case of the older children in this age band, choose not to."[5]

**Eleven to fourteen years:** This is typically an era characterized by hormones as puberty strikes, and the emphasis for children moves largely from home and the family towards the external world, their peers, and "idols" in the quest to become "independent". This means a shift from parental identification to peer identification, requiring a degree of experimentation that may involve taking risks. Brain changes cause an inherent drive to seek out social experiences: "these are more likely to be sought in the digital world as we restrict children's and young people's access to outdoor, offline socialisation." Children and young people may start to actively seek out age-restricted material and games that are designed for adults, so keep the communication channels open for discussions of risk and challenging content.

**Fifteen to eighteen years:** In Western culture this is officially the last stage of "childhood", when young people are still the responsibility of their parents but take increasing responsibility for their own decisions and identities. Abstract thinking is likely to be well developed, and evaluation of information and making judgments is becoming more balanced as young people develop their own set of values and beliefs (which may be different from their parents'), for which space should be allowed. This is a good opportunity for young people to experiment with different roles and identities, and make decisions for themselves, while still within the safety of family support.

### Legal limits?

It seems clear that children are starting to go onto the internet at a younger and younger age. Many sites, including Facebook and Twitter, state in their terms of agreement that no under-thirteens are permitted on them. This is tied in particularly with US laws that forbid the collection of data from children under thirteen, but also reflects child development theories that suggest that children are not emotionally developed enough to engage in a healthy manner before this age. In the UK, Australia, and elsewhere there is *no legal reason* why thirteen years should be the minimum age, but children will be breaking site terms and conditions if they join.

. . . . . . . . . . . . . . . . . . . . . . . . . . . . . . . . . . . . . .

No. I have no idea at which age [social networks] are appropriate. This is not because they are "new" or "digital"; I also have no idea at what age I should start giving her pocket money or leave her at home alone for any time. I guess this is a combination of understanding our own particular child and her needs and capabilities, and balancing this with social pressure and the judgments of other parents and indeed society and its laws. But certainly, if it has not been superseded I imagine she will be on Facebook before thirteen – with some level of help/supervision/guidance – and I don't see that as a negative.

**(Parent, 3 to 5)**

The CHILDWISE "Digital Lives" Report 2010 noted that children encountered different degrees of parental involvement in joining Facebook. Some children used their parents' page and then set up their own with parental support; another child set up an account after asking their parents' permission, while yet another child set up an account before asking permission. Some did not tell their parents at all. The report highlighted that although many parents knew there was an age restriction on Facebook, they thought that eleven was a more appropriate age (this was echoed in a range of answers in the questionnaire).

For those who do choose to allow their children to join before thirteen (and it's worth thinking about what message this sends about abiding by rules and regulations), it's worth setting the privacy settings high. Know your child's password, check whom they are friends with, and ensure (through discussion) that they are using Facebook appropriately.

*Questionnaire respondents were asked if they would place age limits on the use of any particular technologies:*

. . . . . . . . . . . . . . . . . . . . . . . . . . . . . . . . . . .

I have already said no to my nine-year-old using Facebook and will not let him join under thirteen, although I know of a number of young people (under thirteen) at church and school who are on it.

**(Parent, 6 to 9)**

. . . . . . . . . . . . . . . . . . . . . . . . . . . . . . . . . . .

At the moment my daughter is only three, so everything she does is supervised. She does enjoy looking at Facebook with me; I suspect when she is older, but less than thirteen, she will want her own account. I'm not sure how we will deal with that, as I think if she was just interacting with friends/family that would be OK… but it's not possible to guarantee that (however, given that she would have to claim to be thirteen, then we wouldn't let her).

**(Parent, 3 to 5)**

. . . . . . . . . . . . . . . . . . . . . . . . . . . . . . . . . . .

I would not allow my child to have Facebook/Twitter, etc. accounts until they were at secondary school at the very earliest. Of course, if "all my friends" actually *had* done so before then, that *might* change. I wouldn't want my children to have phones until secondary school either, but can see that there would be significant peer pressure to have a smartphone as soon as they have a phone of any kind.

**(Parent, 3 to 5, 6 to 9)**

Since there was no way I could prevent them from accessing Facebook/Bebo, etc. elsewhere than at home at any age, I decided they could use Facebook when they asked to (about eleven years old), and I explained the risks and dangers and the security/privacy measures necessary.

**(Parent, 19 or over)**

I didn't allow my eldest to use FB until she was thirteen, which was just into her second year at secondary school. My other daughter was born in July and it seems hard to make her wait until she has finished her second year before letting her on FB. Many of her friends are on it, so I will probably allow her soon; I know more about FB now so am better able to help her stay safe.

**(Parent, 10 to 12, 13 to 15)**

Facebook has admitted that it is powerless to stop underage users signing up.[6] This highlights a bigger problem online: children are pretending to be sixteen- or eighteen-year-olds to get around the restrictions, and therefore are exposed to unsuitable material. Research shows that this problem is increasing, and there are, as yet, no effective technological measures in place to deal with it.

## Privacy and permanency

### Password creation

*To ensure that everything you do online is accessible only to those you choose to share it with, you need to have good passwords. Parents should emphasize to children that these shouldn't be given to their friends. If the friendship breaks down, then the ex-friends may decide to post horrible stuff from their account, for which your child will appear to be responsible.*

*Think carefully about the passwords you use, as the CHILDWISE survey (2010) highlighted that children often give up when they forget their login details.*

- *CNN's list of the worst passwords 2012: http://edition.cnn.com/2012/10/25/tech/web/worst-passwords-2012*
- *Looking for a complex password: http://strongpasswordgenerator.com*

*Some of the most effective passwords can be like these (although preferably a little longer) as these are harder to crack:*

- *Sentences where the initial letters become the password: Don't Throw The Baby Out With The Bathwater becomes DTTBOWTB*
- *Letters are substituted with numbers: Jemima15 becomes J3m1ma15*

When you are using the internet, or advising your children, consider your privacy. Mark Zuckerberg, the man behind Facebook, has said that privacy is "no longer a social norm".[7] This can be seen from the way that Facebook encourages us to connect with more and more people, in order to enable them to continue to draw in advertising (which funds their business model). The web is a place that "rewards openness": assume that everything you write online is potentially for public consumption (in the same way as anything that is written on paper could be photocopied and shared, or spoken and recorded). Don't get paranoid and refuse to share, but establish your criteria. Mine would be: Am I happy for my parents to see this? Or any children I work with? Would I mind seeing it on the front page of a newspaper (or shared publicly around Twitter, as Randi Zuckerberg did[8])? Could my worst enemy do anything with what I've written? None of this should *stop* you posting, but it should cause you to *pause and think*. Just because you can, doesn't always mean that you should.

Any technological privacy controls, as always, need to be accompanied by appropriate and aware online behaviour, and an understanding of content-sharing etiquette. All users need to learn how to set privacy settings well and avoid posting material that could be used against them or someone else, including information that could be used for burglary or identity theft. Another issue is that of managing permissions from external apps that you may install. Do ensure, as a parent, that if you do feel your child has over-shared, you hold back on the anger. Otherwise they may just create a mirror profile that you can't see (although a lack of activity will probably raise suspicions, and necessitate another conversation).

· · · · · · · · · · · · · · · · · · · · · · · · · · · · · · · · · · · ·

We have reminded them about safety measures such as not giving away their age, address, etc. We have the restrictions set on our internet connections, and my husband is "friends" with them on FB so sees their postings generally.

**(Parent, 10 to 12, 13 to 15)**

Facebook has appeared in the press several times as its privacy settings are by default quite open, and can be hard to find and change. Many people believe young people don't care about privacy, but research has demonstrated that they do[9] and are largely confident about managing their privacy settings, with less than 1 per cent describing the process on Facebook as "very difficult".[10] Some also feel that online spaces offer more safety, privacy, and control than offline ones (especially if they share a room), with one girl (fourteen to fifteen) saying, "The real world's not that safe, is it?"[11] Other organizations, such as the BBC, give good advice on how they are responsible for children's information.[12]

## Monitoring

Many parents use software[13] or other tactics to monitor what their children are viewing online, in an era in which constant vigilance appears to be required in order to qualify as a good parent. Children now, however, access the internet via so many different devices, without a single access point, that it is much harder for parents to know exactly what their children are doing, although not all agree that this is necessary.

· · · · · · · · · · · · · · · · · · · · · · · · · · · · · · · · · · · · ·

Children learn best by doing. Maybe I'm fortunate in having sensible girls as my kids, but I'd rather give them the freedom to explore (with a risk of getting hurt along the way by getting it wrong) than try to control their online life too much. Let's face it: I'm not present at most of their face-to-face conversations with their peers, so why should I be overseeing their online conversations? I do discuss safety issues with them a lot, though.

**(Parent, 10 to 12, 13 to 15)**

· · · · · · · · · · · · · · · · · · · · · · · · · · · · · · · · · · · · ·

I do think it is harder to monitor his mobile phone usage and history and it is very easy for digital content that I would not approve of to be viewed via his phone.

**(Parent, 6 to 9, 16 to 18)**

Although frustrated by their parents' "spying", children accept they are acting out of the best intentions, to protect them from potential external threats, and know they can rely on their parents to help if they encounter any pitfalls. This open approach to monitoring is definitely the most helpful, in contrast to undercover "spying", which Linda Blair, a clinical psychologist and author of *The Happy Child*, feels is incredibly damaging to the trust required for effective communication with a child.[14]

*Following a survey of children, uKnowKids highlighted the top ten behaviours that they found embarrassing if they were "friends" with their parents on Facebook. The headings were as follows:*[15]

 *1. Posting Too Much*

 *2. "Liking" Every Post*

 *3. Using Outdated Slang*

 *4. Tagging Embarrassing Pictures*

 *5. Sending "Friend" Requests to Their Friends*

 *6. Using Their Wall as a Form of Communication*

 *7. Being Too Personal*

 *8. Fighting Their Kids' Battles*

 *9. Correcting Poor Grammar or Spelling Mistakes*

 *10. Posting for Their Kids.*

- - - - - - - - - - - - - - - - - - - - - - - - - - - - - - - - - -

We are "friends" on Facebook with our children. At first our daughter used our email account for Facebook notifications, which enabled us to be aware of what she was doing. As she has got older, this has changed.

**(Parent, 13 to 15, 16 to 18)**

Some parents insist on having their child's login details and checking their Facebook activity, or on being Facebook friends, in the hope that this will encourage their children to think twice before posting, in case the parent is watching. If you do this, you may find that their friends choose to connect with you, but even if they don't, ensure you don't humiliate your child by what you post on their wall, and don't forget that they can choose to limit what you can see. It may be worth checking with the parents of your children's friends if they make a "friend" request. Remember also that your children can see what you are doing![16]

> I have always made it clear that these things are
> a privilege, not a right, and can be removed at any
> time. She has always understood that this is to keep
> her safe, not to be controlling or mean. Keeping
> passwords secret and limiting access to communal
> areas of the house are essential. Most of all,
> keeping open lines of communication and discussing
> her friends' online activity are important.
>
> **(Parent, 13 to 15)**

It's important to keep all this in perspective, particularly once your child is officially an adult. The story of the Irelands, who were illegally monitoring their twenty-one-year-old daughter's computing activity when she went off to university, demonstrates what happens when it all goes horribly wrong: they were issued with a restraining order for a year.[17]

### Filtering

Some parents may wish to use filtering software on computers,[18] but this should come with a couple of warnings. It's not 100 per cent effective at blocking material (and in fact will probably block material that you *do* want to see), and it is most effective if done in conjunction with your child. As the number of children possessing mobile devices grows, mobile companies are developing child-friendly filtering software, but if your child hooks into free Wi-Fi, as provided in most outlets, all those protections disappear. It may be worth investing in safety software for younger children, limiting their time online, controlling who they can communicate privately with, reviewing their search histories, and providing a safe play area. Those thinking they can use this on teens, however, just need to Google "bypass internet filter"!

We bought Net Nanny®. We uninstalled it two months
later as it wouldn't let her see websites she
genuinely needed to do her school homework. We tried
to have the discussion about online safety and were
more successful talking about identity protection
than unsavoury pornographic sites, which were too
difficult and embarrassing to raise. My wife was
better about talking this through than I was.

**(Parent, 19 or over)**

I find it incredible that my security settings
blocked a sermon from Holy Trinity Brompton as
inappropriate but allowed my seven-year-old to
play a game that involved killing parents and
children with blades and "blood". Better security
is required, and a better definition of appropriate/
inappropriate content, particularly from what I can
see on game sites and YouTube.

**(Parent, 6 to 9, 13 to 15)**

In choosing your software, you can select whether the product
creates a blacklist (it blocks sites based upon specific keywords),
or a white list (it only allows sites that you authenticate). Some
software allows children to "request access", and you can
decide whether to allow this or not. Journalist Pamela Whitby
tested a range of filtering products, and found that across the
board, an average of 20 per cent of harmful content wasn't
blocked. So if you are going to use filtering tools, they need
to be part of the bigger picture, including if you add Google
SafeSearch.[19] Mumsnet, based upon its user group, suggests:
Google SafeSearch; CyberPatrol™; Net Nanny®; Windows
Vista; Mac OS X as best for blocking questionable websites
and monitoring time online.[20] The BBC also offers options for
locking down their content.[21]

At the time of writing a hot topic for legislative discussions was whether to filter at source, requiring opt-in to "adult" sites, but this was strongly challenged by "free speech" advocates, and in 2012, an automatic block on porn was rejected.[22] In August 2013, however, British Prime Minister David Cameron reintroduced the idea.[23]

· · · · · · · · · · · · · · · · · · · · · · · · · · · · · · · · · ·

Parental controls on email are particularly good. I can set things up so they can only send and receive emails from certain people, which allows them some freedom.

**(Parent, 6 to 9, 10 to 12)**

· · · · · · · · · · · · · · · · · · · · · · · · · · · · · · · · · ·

I strongly feel it is essential for the government to support parents in this by making ISPs responsible for setting pornographic and other harmful sites (e.g. extreme violence, etc.) as opt-in only sites. This would be extremely helpful.

**(Carer, 13 to 15)**

CHILDWISE, Ofcom, and the EU Kids Online research has all demonstrated that only a minority of parents install filtering software, with most preferring soft monitoring, especially amidst hectic lives, and the increasing mobility of devices. Byron, in her 2010 progress review, re-emphasized that filtering by default (as the government has been considering) would give parents a false sense of security, and parents need to understand how to set up controls more effectively, combining this with discussions about digital safety.

Most parents want to protect their children from porn, as this parent highlights:

· · · · · · · · · · · · · · · · · · · · · · · · · · · · · · · · · ·

At a friend's house one of our daughters inadvertently came across a pornographic site

because she and her friend Googled "Big Ben" wanting
pictures of Westminster — perhaps other families'
computers are not switched to safe settings?
**(Parent, 6 to 9, 10 to 12)**

A report in *The Guardian* in February 2013 listed various things that had upset children, including online violence, "someone swearing at me", "a picture of my baby brother, who I don't live with any more", and a picture of a cat that "looked like my pet that had to be put down". Professor Phippen, writing the report for the UK Council for Child Internet Safety, said: "There is no silver bullet to crack child safety online. The Government's obsession with filtering is OK, but too narrow."[24]

*Consider using the "Hector's World Safety Button", which allows your child to press a button to cover the screen so that they don't have to continue viewing anything distressing while they go to get help: http://www.thinkuknow.co.uk/5_7/hectorsworld/Hectors-World-Safety-Button1/*

## Location services

The growing popularity of smartphones and the development of software options such as "Facebook Places" have made it easier, and more likely, that children will sign in to the locations they are in. The CHILDWISE Report 2012 noted that the numbers of children using "check-in" services had more than doubled over the previous year, and that less opposition was voiced. A particular appeal was the ability to discover where friends were in order to be able to join them. CHILDWISE noted that boys and girls were equally as likely to use the software, but girls were more likely to say they would never use it.

We have covered some of the following points before, but it's important to reiterate the essential questions to consider when it comes to location information, which are:

- Can people find out exactly where you are, right now?
- Can people locate where one of your friends is because you've checked them in?
- Can people work out your regular routine from your check-ins?
- Can people tell where you are *not*, because you've checked in elsewhere?

Although I have good neighbours who keep an eye on my property when I'm away, I never check in at home or take photos of the outside of my house, because, with my job, it is always very clear when I am somewhere else.

## Managing your digital fingerprint

Headlines such as those about Paris Brown, forced to stand down from her role with the police because of a racist tweet sent two years before, resonate with parents.[25] Every interaction that we make online leaves a trail, commonly known as a "digital footprint", which others, such as future employers, may find on searching for your child's name. Other terms are also used, such as "digital shadow". I prefer the idea of a "digital fingerprint" – our opportunity to make a unique and personal contribution online, rather than "stomping all over the net", although I've also been heard to say that "1s and 0s, the building blocks of the digital world, never forget".

Eric Schmidt, CEO of Google, believes that parents need to have the "online privacy" talk before they have the "sex talk" with their child, and also warns that parents should think about the names they give their children. The more unique a name, the easier it is to find – which could be viewed as both an advantage and a disadvantage.[26]

The Parenting Place in New Zealand notes that many parents are announcing their pregnancy online (around 25 per cent share the news via the first scan), posting the child's birth, first words, and first steps, creating a digital shadow before the child is even born. By the time they're two, more than 90 per cent of children have an online history. A new term, "Sharents", has been created for parents who appear to share every moment of their child's life.[27] Mashable gives some useful advice to such parents, and to those trying to cope with the "baby overload": don't believe that others have "perfect lives" with their children.[28]

A major concern for many parents is the "permanent" nature of anything posted online, and the effect that may have upon future employability. With the growth of technology, including smartphones and Google Glass, it has become easier and easier to capture every aspect of life. In the past, if you made a fool of yourself at a party, it was gradually forgotten about, but with digital technology it could be all over Facebook or Twitter before you get home, and you have to think about how to live with that:

• • • • • • • • • • • • • • • • • • • • • • • • • • • • • • • • •

… anything shared on Twitter is public, searchable, instant and permanent.

**(Parent, 19 or over)**

Writing in 2008, Don Tapscott, the author who created the term "Net Generation", highlighted a UK survey which revealed that 62 per cent of British employers check the social networking posts of potential employees, with 25 per cent rejecting candidates on that basis. His son Alex, however, thinks employers should relax, although his friends tend to agree on a no-picture-tagging policy when out with friends:

*If there's a photo of me drinking a beer at a party what does that say about me – that I'm a bad potential hire who abuses alcohol, or alternatively that I'm a social person who likes to enjoy life, with friends and a good network?*[29]

**EXERCISE: Try a Google search of your child's name, and its variations (consider doing this with your child). Check variations of your name; for example, I would look for "Rebecca Lewis" as well as "Bex Lewis".**

**Encourage your child to think about what their profile would look like if an alien landed and just had their social media to read.**

**List the types of information they are sharing, the issues associated with sharing, and the appropriate actions that should be taken to avoid problems arising.**

Dan Tynan is a contributing editor with *Family Circle*, where he writes about the intersection of parenting and technology.[30] He decided to search for his son online, using variations of his name and some digital identities he knew of. Some of the information was incorrect, and he worked with Google to remove the offending data.[31]

It's not necessary to see a "digital fingerprint" as something negative. Don't think that you don't have one – we all do, but we can take control of it, and fill the online spaces with positive information. If children wait until they are leaving school and ready to start looking for work, it's too late to have developed a decent online profile (although better late than never). Search engines take time to "crawl" through content online, sometimes up to six months for new material from an unknown site – although I've also put a post up, searched for the term sixty seconds later, and seen it returned as the top entry.

# 7

# Identity: Values and Authenticity

Sherry Turkle, Professor of the Social Studies of Science and Technology at MIT, speaks of Mona (fourteen), who, once allowed to join Facebook, wanted to write the "real me", but found the "real me" to be elusive. She edited and re-edited her profile, deciding what to include or exclude, which pictures to use, and whether to "look good" or to give an insight into "troubled times". What if her life wasn't interesting enough, and at what point in a relationship should it become "Facebook official"? In 2013, research was conducted into self-censorship of status updates (those deleted before posting, based on 3.9 million Facebook users). Around a third of messages were deleted before publication. Some of the reasons given were that:

- it might offend or hurt someone
- it might be boring or repetitive
- it might undermine their desired self-presentation
- some were unable to post because of technological problems
- they were worried that it might spark an argument.[1]

I would question, however, how much of this is simply a part of the usual editing process, which is helpful to go through before committing to the "Publish" button.

Media Studies lecturer Marcus Leaning refers to the huge amount of early research that concentrated on online identity, which was heavily focused on the loss of face-to-face clues, and on deceit. These academic attitudes have filtered down into everyday thinking and continue to feature in the press, and help us understand why online identity remains such a huge concern to parents.[2] Thinking back to the exercise on "values", encourage children to seek to define their identity online according to internal values, whether they believe they are anonymous or not. This *does not* mean they need to tell everyone everything, especially when encouraged to do so on the social networks!

Developmental theories tend to assume that, in adolescence, young people are driven to experiment with their identities and self-presentation, and the online world adds a new element to this. Professor David Buckingham refers to the fact that young people revisit what they have produced online, not only to update it but to see the kind of response they have received, and that they adapt what they produce according to feedback.[3] A huge part of the Bailey Review is concerned with images produced *in* the media, as was seen in the terrible barrage of tweets to the French tennis player Marion Bartoli, many of which appear to have been sent by teenagers, related to her appearance on winning Wimbledon in 2013.[4] This is supported by Dr Linda Papadopoulos, a psychologist who contributed to the Bailey Review:

*From digital citizenship to media literacy, equipping kids with tools to help them understand and interpret what they see without internalizing all the negative messages can help them build their self-esteem and inner confidence so they feel secure in their own identity. Just as they are taught reading comprehension and, later, literary criticism, children can be taught how to critique the media they consume.[5]*

In 2003 a survey was conducted of 800 children in three secondary schools who were ordinary users, rather than the extreme users that most research had previously concentrated on. This survey noted that teenagers are particularly conscious of how others observe them as their bodies develop, and that computers give more control over the pace of conversation, and no blushes can be seen.[6] Online spaces are particularly useful for working through identities such as lesbian, gay, or disabled, as online relationships tend to be based on shared interests rather than accidents of geography, and it's easier to find others in the same situation. It's also possible to find relief from the structured round of activities that so many children are involved in, and to pursue their own passions and interests, at their own pace. One parent discovered not only that her daughter wanted to learn to play the guitar, but that she had already started learning via YouTube tutorials.[7]

## Role models

As young people develop their identities they need guidance and support, particularly from the significant adults in their lives. The behaviour that those adults model, whether it's with regard to digital technologies or great historical events such as the Holocaust, or even in the way the cleaner is treated, is important in helping children define their own identity, values, and attitudes.

Elaine Halligan of The Parent Practice warns that 80 per cent of parenting is modelling: "If your mobile is surgically attached to your hip 24/7, don't be surprised if your teenagers have trouble letting go."[8] A friend of mine said their child would bring their phone to them, as this was what seemed to get the most attention. They made a decision to put all phones down at the door, at least until the child went to bed. This is echoed by "Playground Dad", who says:

*Put the phone away and be a dad. While this is the hardest to do, it's the most important. The emails, tweets, and sport scores will be there when the crew is in bed. Most dads don't think kids take notice, but after listening to my students, I can say they do notice and it's not in a positive way.*[9]

Even if you think that your child is engrossed in their device so it's OK to be on yours, they may just be waiting for you to give them some attention, or for you to impose some boundaries.

*Randi Zuckerberg, author of* The New York Times *bestseller* Dot Complicated: Untangling Our Wired Lives: *"Even at such a young age, Asher gets visibly frustrated when I use my phone while playing with him. I have to unplug more than I did before I was a mom, so I can give him my undivided attention, which is crucial for early childhood development. In fact I actually find I need to monitor my own tech usage more than I need to create rules around his. Kids model their behavior after their parents'. It's easy to tell our children to turn off their phones by 7 p.m., but if we really want them to listen, we need to heed the same advice. How many times have you answered work emails at the dinner table? We are raising our children to think it's perfectly acceptable to have our smartphones at arm's (and eye's) reach at all times. In the end, our goal is to teach our children to use technology responsibly, rather than technology dictating their lives."*[10]

Bad behaviour has been exhibited by adults, with a 2013 US survey establishing that 60 per cent of all adults are texting and driving (most of whom wouldn't have done so three years ago), despite knowing that it's exceptionally dangerous. This *Mashable* article then provides some recommendations for apps to put a phone into "drive mode", or to allow parents to track their children's style of driving.[11]

**EXERCISE: Take time with your child to think of/ discuss strong/positive role models, and what they are contributing as role models.**

## Anonymity

Online, there is an expectation that people can be invisible, through the creation of fake profiles and secondary anonymous emails (extra accounts created with the express purpose of the sender remaining unknown), although, with determination, anyone's identity can be found out. The term used here is "disinhibition", which occurs when the technology appears to offer a buffer from traditional consequences. People will say and do things online that they would not otherwise say or do, because they have lost the clues of the feedback cycle.

Disinhibition can have positive consequences, enabling the shy to speak up and providing a space to ask questions that would otherwise be too difficult to ask. It can also have negative consequences and allow people to engage in hurtful behaviour, hidden behind a false identity. In the US, a series of sites such as JuicyCampus, and now Facebook pages, allow users to post anonymously, which can open up some great discussions, but they are also plagued with hate talk.[12]

# 8

# Relationships (Online)

In this chapter, we will look at how children and youth use and benefit from digital relationships. Friends are seen as children's most precious resource, so they will therefore devote a lot of time to building those relationships.

. . . . . . . . . . . . . . . . . . . . . . . . . . . . . . . . .

[Our children] show great creativity; they are very up to date with their knowledge and they are incredibly sociable – they keep in contact with a greater range of friends and acquaintances than we were ever able to, across many diverse and widespread networks. They actually keep us parents better informed about their whereabouts than I ever did my parents(!).
**(Parent, 16 to 18, 19 or over)**

Although in practice most children are continuing conversations with friends from their local area, it's fascinating to see how often "online" communication is viewed as second-rate, as we see from Professor Livingstone's comment:

*Even though ... face-to-face communication can... be angry, negligent, resistant, deceitful and inflexible, somehow it remains the ideal against which mediated communication is judged as flawed.*[1]

The online spaces do add a new dynamic to these relationships. Sherry Turkle, MIT academic and author of *Alone Together*, highlights how things have changed. In Victorian times you called round and left a "calling card", with no expectation about whether you'd be seen. Now, with Facebook, you send a "friend request", but the rules are not clear about who should be accepted. How many friends are too many? How much will those who have been refused be upset? If you refuse someone from school, how will that affect your offline interactions? How much do you have to engage once you're on Facebook? Do you have to give everyone the same level of interaction?[2]

## Friendships

Now Senior Researcher at Microsoft Research, danah boyd[3] studied MySpace when it was *the* social networking site to be on. Teenagers joined because that was where their pre-existing friendship group was, and then just "hung out".[4] Once online, many children have had to learn the etiquette for the new space, and it's perfectly acceptable to "lurk" for a while and see what others are doing. Most join because someone invites them, and then they have to decide whom to "friend". Some friends are added because it would be socially awkward to say no, because it makes the teenager look cool, or because the befriender thinks it would be interesting to read their posts. Ito Mizuko, a cultural anthropologist at the University of California, identified that because it's awkward to say no to those who are already known, the convention is to accept all those who are known, regardless of the quality of the relationship.[5]

Professor Robin Dunbar, a British anthropologist, famously said that it's possible to maintain only 150 "meaningful" friendships,[6] which causes parents to worry that their children are therefore not investing in "meaningful" relationships because they have "thousands" of online friends. As someone with several thousand online connections, I'm not convinced: what does "meaningful" mean? Social media can be used more as an address book, with privacy settings allowing access to different levels of information, while the public parade of connections offers social identity and status. "Friends" is a term that is used fairly loosely, covering a wide range of connections. Teenagers would say that it's OK to have many connections, but describe their peers who simply seek to "collect" friends (without true connections) as "whores".[7]

One noticeable difference in the digital era, especially as the social platforms have stabilized, is that it's difficult to leave anyone behind, which can be delicate to negotiate:

*Generally, it is socially unacceptable to delete a Friend one knows. When this is done, it is primarily after a fight or breakup. In these situations, the act of deletion is spiteful and intentionally designed to hurt the other person.*[8]

Teens know this, so if someone is accidentally deleted, it can be problematic. MySpace made this harder by forcing people to publicly choose their eight "top friends". Ito Mizuko notes that all the elements of offline relationships, including gossiping, bullying, and jockeying for status, continue online, but "are also reshaped in significant ways because of the new forms of publicity and always-on communication". Significant energies are put into "hanging out", building friendships, and taking time to "play", which adults don't always see as particularly constructive, but which is central to the developmental experience.[9]

Not all children, however, have the time, resources or space to play, so certain groups (usually those with more money) can become privileged. The ability to be fully engaged also requires sociability and the ability to be "on call", thus improving opportunities for superior social status. Many expect an instant response and become irritated or worried if someone from their peer group doesn't reply at once, especially if it can be seen that they are online, although this is behaviour that I've noticed *across the age groups*.

As we have seen, much has been made of the fact that social media allow children to connect with others outside their geographical friendship groups, including those coping with disability or coming to terms with their sexuality. Being online does give them a chance to talk "anonymously" without immediate social consequences, but Ito Mizuko reports that "teens often use social media to make or develop friendships, but they do so almost exclusively with acquaintances or friends of friends".[10] She further notes that there's a bit of a stigma about making friends online, made worse by the perception that meeting people online is dangerous.[11] This was written in 2009, however, and I would say that it's now become more acceptable, if appropriate care is taken.

*Sit down with your child and ask them to take you to their social networking profile and go through every single friend to whom they are linked. Ask them to tell you who each one is and how they know them. Explain that one of the reasons you are doing this is because whilst it is not a good idea anyway for children to have perfect strangers on their buddy list now these new location apps have arrived it makes that more important than ever. Be ready to explain why but without scaring them out of their wits! (John Carr OBE)*[12]

### Image tagging

A core element of friendship online is the sharing and "tagging" of photos. According to Nielsen research, Instagram was the top photography site among twelve- to seventeen-year-olds, with 1 million teens visiting the site during July 2012, unlike the general population, which still prioritized Flickr.[13] Take time to talk to your child about what kind of information they give away about themselves in photos (e.g. school uniform), and encourage them to ask their friends' permission before posting photos of others. With the increasing sophistication of facial recognition software (which compares new images with pre-existing tagged images online), there's a growing chance of being tagged, although the Canadian MediaSmarts research (2012) demonstrated that most of their participants were savvy enough to regulate their own image, routinely untagging themselves in images on Facebook, and requesting friends to take down unflattering pictures. As a last resort they have reported those that they wish to have removed, or removed them themselves. They monitored friends' pages to ensure that they were being represented fairly, and trusted each other not to expose silly or embarrassing pictures. Those that were on the phone were considered to be private and not for sharing without agreement, although children should still consider what might happen to those photos if the friendship were to fall apart.

Research shows that most teen social media users agree that they love posting photos of themselves online, with three-quarters of girls and nearly half the boys feeling that way, with a significant number seeking approval in the form of "Likes". One thing that many users are not aware of is that most smartphones attach a huge amount of information to photos, including geolocation – right down to the detail of a specific room. This is very easy to switch off in the settings, and worth doing in places where you routinely hang out and at home.[14]

**EXERCISE: Take time (eighteen minutes) to watch http:// cybersmart.gov.au/tagged, a video produced for Australian schools (designed for children fourteen+), demonstrating how the mix of online and offline can allow a joke to get**

**out of hand, with a simple photo tag leading to problems
that follow the student from school to school. Discuss the
issues that are raised, and potential solutions.**

*Facebook depression?*

A recent academic study concluded that witnessing friends'
holidays, love lives, and work successes on Facebook can lead to
strong feelings of envy, leaving people feeling lonely, frustrated,
and angry.[15] This can be particularly difficult for mums, who
think that everyone else is being "supermum": everyone seems
to be having a better life![16] Some teenagers would say we have
to get a grip on this: "My life looks better on the Internet than
it does in real life. Everyone's life looks better on the Internet
than it does in real life. The Internet is partial truths – we get to
decide what people see and what they don't."[17]

The American Academy of Paediatrics claims this can lead
to clinical depression, but parents should not fear, as other
research demonstrates that, for most, Facebook and other social
networking sites have the opposite effect of making users feel
less depressed.[18] Overall, teens report a high degree of well-
being, and no difference was found between those who are
heavy users of social networking sites and others. Ferguson,
a professor from Texas A&M University who researches the
technologies' effects on human behaviour, claims: "Youth today
are the least aggressive, most civically involved, and mentally
well in several generations."[19]

## Cyberbullying

Taking that on board, let's tackle another controversial issue,
which has featured in frequent newspaper headlines. There
have been high-profile cases, such as that of Megan Meier, who
committed suicide after enduring extensive bullying online.[20]
Rehtaeh Parsons also committed suicide after photos of her
being raped were circulated globally,[21] and Olympic diver Tom

Daley was taunted in 2012.[22] In early 2013, *The New York Times* noted that there's been a huge surge in anti-bullying books (something I discovered in my research for this book), spurred on in part by these high-profile cases. Several of these books are designed for parents to read together with their children, and they don't necessarily all have happy endings.[23]

In all of this, we have to remember that these are the worst-case scenarios, tragic in every case but usually more complex than the headlines would have us believe. Social networking may be a factor, but it's not the only one. We need to accept this if we want society to look for the right solutions to the problem, particularly ensuring that our own children are not tempted to become bullies themselves, or to stand by while others do the bullying.

• • • • • • • • • • • • • • • • • • • • • • • • • • • • • • • • • •

The usual problems that children have always had in relating to other children (bullying, harassment, exclusion), [are] now transferred to a digital arena.

**(Grandparents, 6 to 9)**

### *Statistics and the particular nature of online bullying*

The core difference between "traditional" bullying and "online" bullying is the nature of it. Previously, bullying would typically stop at the school gates, or at least once the child got home, although there was always the potential for phone calls, notes falling out of homework books, bricks through the window, or events replaying themselves in the mind. Online bullying, however, can be constant, happening any time of day and night, affecting the child regardless of location, including at home, and leaving a feeling that there is nowhere to escape to. The other particular characteristic of online bullying is that it is much easier for others to get involved quickly. It rapidly collects and remains permanently in cyberspace, rather than being a spur-of-the-moment action. It is therefore difficult to obtain "closure" because at any time the information might resurface and another episode of bullying, with accompanying public humiliation, could kick off.

. . . . . . . . . . . . . . . . . . . . . . . . . . . . . . . . . . . . . . .

I am concerned about the ability of some digital tools to amplify and broaden the kinds of thoughtless and/or mean-spirited peer-to-peer interactions that might at one time have existed in a scrawled note.

**(Parent, 10 to 12)**

Vodafone quoted research from the Family Online Safety Institute (FOSI) which indicates that at least two-thirds of teenagers have had positive experiences online, although most had witnessed mean behaviour to others, and less than a fifth reported being a target.[24] Bullying is of particular concern to parents because of the emotional harm it can do and the way it can affect self-esteem, confidence, and school attendance and performance, and therefore overall life chances. Although the 2010 statistics for online-only bullying (6 per cent) are much lower than "traditional" bullying (19 per cent), the effects are felt more intensely, hence the huge concern about online bullying in particular.[25] I was intrigued to see that, having shared the first few paragraphs of this section on Facebook, multiple people piled in with their experiences and suggestions of what was different, and how much impact bullying had had on their lives (even pre-digitally).

**EXERCISE: Choose a video related to bullying (some examples here), and use it as a conversation starter with your children:**

- **http://youtu.be/ltun92DfnPY (7:36, animation, "To This Day Project": see the backstory: http://youtu.be/sa1iS1MqUy4)**
- **http://youtu.be/-5PZ_Bh-M60 (4:40, drama, The "Cyber Bullying Virus")**
- **http://youtu.be/2YGjz5SV_Qk (5:37, drama, for those "just watching")**
- **http://youtu.be/40Z0a41zsZA (3:19, interview, Simon's parents)**

Bullying, in its traditional form, involves aggressive and repeated actions over time by individuals or a group against a chosen victim. Cyberbullying adds a layer enabled through technology, most often via mobile phones. Parents need to be particularly aware of it between the ages of thirteen and sixteen, when there's a noticeable peak in cyberbullying. The older child is more typically the perpetrator, although there are an increasing number taking the roles of both victim and bully, using the internet as a space to seek revenge, particularly on someone physically bigger.

*ITV reported in February 2013:*
- *More than two-thirds of children say they have received abusive messages from someone they know.*
- *Almost half of youngsters keep the attack secret.*
- *One in five think sending a message in cyberspace is less damaging than face-to-face insults.*
- *Half the teenagers polled believe it is OK to say things online that you would not in person.*
- *A third of youths say they troll because their friends do so too.*[26]

### Terminology
In view of all this concern, a huge number of surveys have been undertaken, which place the numbers of those affected at

anywhere between 5.5 per cent and 71 per cent! It is important to dig beneath these statistics to truly understand what we're dealing with, as they affect government policies, school policies, and decisions that we make, individually and as a part of our communities, as parents. The higher the statistics, the more likely we are to limit children's online access and buy into a "surveillance culture".

The 2012 Vodafone *Digital Parenting* magazine noted that many children lose interest when we talk about "bullying", because they often refer to what happens as "drama", of which the imbalance of power that is crucial to bullying is not necessarily a part. MediaSmarts identified a feeling that schools and parents being so quick to term what teenagers would regard as a "normal" part of their everyday communication as "bullying" was unhelpful.[27] Bullying is more serious and harmful than this everyday conversation, and is characterized by deliberate, repeated, and hostile behaviour. Cyberbullying expert Dr Shaheen Shariff would argue that government and the media have defined bullying as a "thing", "controlled, managed and packaged, bucketed and blueprinted",[28] as this makes us feel that it's easier to deal with, but this can stop us, as a society, from looking in the right direction for solutions.

*Some types of cyberbullying:*
- *Threatening or hateful text, email or chat messages.*
- *Pictures or video clips, including "happy slapping".*
- *Silent or abusive phone calls.*
- *Stealing a phone, and using it to harass others.*
- *Nasty comments posted on websites or social media.*
- *Blogging to damage the reputation or privacy of others, including sharing personal data.*
- *Creating internet polls such as "Who's hot".*
- *Forcing users to share messages, threatening "social isolation" for non-compliance.*

*Risk factors*

Headlines such as "Schoolgirl hangs herself after she's bullied by online trolls"[29] attribute much to the power of social networking alone. Research has highlighted that the factors that lead to bullying online are typically the same as those offline. Although social media may be a catalyst in teen drama, causing it to be spread faster and wider, it's unlikely to be the sole cause of suicide. To label it as such is unhelpful, possibly even dangerous, as it may encourage copycat behaviour from others who feel that they don't get enough attention.

• • • • • • • • • • • • • • • • • • • • • • • • • • • • • • • • •

```
When she is older, I anticipate having some worries
about loss or theft of her phone, the distraction it
affords, and some social issues to do with exclusion
or bullying on social media, e.g. Facebook. However,
these don't seem overwhelming and would have to
be faced in a non-digital world too, and the
benefits far outweigh these concerns from my current
perspective.
```
**(Parent, 3 to 5)**

Those at risk from cyberbullying will tend to be similar to those at risk of offline bullying: they may be physically or mentally challenged, non-heterosexual, highly intelligent or "nerdy" (socially inept), and lacking in self-confidence; they may look or dress differently, or be rule-followers. They may not defend themselves, or may be unaware of the potential danger of bullying so don't nip things in the bud, and they may have poor relationships with parents or caregivers. We have returned, then, to the need for parents to be aware of the characteristics of their own children, and the need to communicate, communicate, communicate!

Within the digital sphere, extra factors that make people more likely to be victims include: being female, being a previous victim of bullying, using chat windows, chatting with older people online, giving away too much personal information online, and giving passwords to others. Girls tend to focus bullying on the areas of appearance and sensuality, and are threatened with stalking or being forced to submit, while boys' bullying tends to focus on sexual orientation or lack of ability, athletic or otherwise, with truly aggressive threats. Ito Mizuko noted particularly that "drama" is often caused if a girl comments or messages someone else's boyfriend, as this is seen as an affront.[30] Dr Shariff noted that boys tended to exhibit anger, but girls showed fear and helplessness. Boys often "took action" and therefore felt they had "dealt with it", although such retaliation tended to lead to another round of bullying.[31]

### Spotting bullying

How do you know if your child is being bullied? Many of the symptoms of bullying can be part of typical adolescent behaviour, so care is required, plus a good knowledge of your child, in order for you to be alert to subtle behavioural changes. Those who have been physically bullied typically exhibit:

- unexplained headaches
- nausea
- bedwetting
- mood swings
- aggression
- night terrors
- falling behind with schoolwork
- avoiding going to school or leaving the house
- becoming antisocial.

Such behaviour can be seen in those who have been cyberbullied too, but extra signs to look out for include:

- long hours on the computer
- secretive internet use

- screen minimization
- refusing to log on or answer phone
- extreme possessiveness of phone, at which constant nervous looks are directed.

Nancy Willard, who runs many cyberbullying workshops in schools, emphasizes that it's important to understand that not "everybody does it", nor is this just a "stage of life" that children have to survive. The media suggestion that there is a cyberbullying epidemic tends to encourage children to think that they can send hurtful messages because "everyone else is doing it". Willard argues that the evidence is that *at some point in their life* 20 per cent have been either a victim or a perpetrator of cyberbullying. There's a real need to collect more information about constructive behaviour online, and share that around, to help young people understand that the majority of people behave positively online.[32]

*Professor Sonia Livingstone and the EU Kids Online team identified a range of coping strategies:*
- *31 per cent tried to solve problems online.*
- *24 per cent simply hoped the problem would go away (not effective).*
- *12 per cent felt guilty about the incidents.*
- *45 per cent sought "personal social support" – friends, parents, siblings, other adults (in that order).*
- *41 per cent deleted messages (which helped).*
- *20 per cent stopped using the internet (which didn't help).*
- *18 per cent changed their filter or contact settings.*
- *9 per cent reported to their internet advisor or service provider, although this was felt to be particularly unsuccessful.*

*Technically blocking the culprit is common and relatively effective.*[33]

*Effective intervention?*

The importance of getting involved early cannot be overstated, and fear-mongering isn't effective. Telling children to "Just ignore it" is not helpful, nor is saying "Just don't go online", as that will simply lead to social isolation. This is not a long-term solution in any way, although stepping aside for a short while can help the child gain some perspective. Bullying is done on purpose, and will be repeated, with four role-players involved: the bully, the target, the bystander who does nothing, and the person who is prepared to step in and stop it. Each of us has to take responsibility for our own part, including tackling others when appropriate. We'll come back to the other roles, but let's look at what happens if your child has become a target.

*A useful slide presentation for parents from uKnowKids: http://www. slideshare.net/uKnowKids/10-essential-things-parents-need-to-know-about-cyberbullying*

Try to keep the communication channels open, but also understand that many children will seek support from their peers if possible. Those who are enabled to deal with the problem, rather than retreat from it, gain confidence to deal with any further incidents. Those who are very upset, are already self-confident, or are long-term victims (so are fed up) are the most likely to head towards action. The most vulnerable are likely to just stay offline, feeling unable to talk to anyone, or to take any action that will make the situation better, and thereby reducing their capacity to cope even further.

The following are some useful steps to take to help your child:

- Ensure they understand that it's not their fault, that they did nothing to draw this upon themselves, and there's no need to feel ashamed.
- Emphasize that they won't lose online access.

- Spend extra time with your child to keep the communication lines open.
- Look for other ways to support and nurture their self-confidence.

Practically:

- Encourage them not to respond, as this rewards the bully.
- Download copies of messages before deleting them, in case they are needed in future.
- Search for "How to block users/accounts" for the platform your child is using, although be aware that the bully may have multiple logins.
- Talk to your child about whether they are happy for you to contact their school (particularly important if their schoolwork is being affected).
- Consider talking to the parents of the bully (if known), although be aware that this can make things worse. If you do decide to take this route, write down the facts, decide what you are going to say, and try to remain calm.
- If illegal information is on another website, contact the web host: they have a legal obligation to remove it.
- Call your network provider to have a particular number blocked.

Kay Stephens, the author of *Cyberslammed*, draws upon years of martial-arts experience to emphasize that to "stand up" to bullies online doesn't necessarily mean you need to fight back. Instead, he says it means to believe in your own dignity, and refuse to allow yourself to become a target again. Before rejoining the online world, those who have been bullied need to think about how they are going to react the next time they are online, and, just as bullies' power comes from their supporters, they should ensure that *they* have support systems in place too. As a parent, don't forget to ask *your* friends for their advice and support.[34]

*Some useful sites for those needing help:*
- *http://www.papyrus-uk.org (preventing young suicide)*
- *http://www.thetrevorproject.org (suicide prevention for LGBTQ [Lesbian, Gay, Bisexual, Transgender, Questioning] youth)*
- *http://www.childline.org.uk/ (confidential helpline for those under nineteen)*
- *http://www.beatbullying.org (advice about cyberbullying, and opportunities to report your own situation, or someone else's)*
- *http://twloha.com/vision (US-based site for those struggling with depression, addiction, self-injury, and suicidal thoughts)*
- *http://www.athinline.org (MTV site for those suffering digital abuse)*
- *http://www.itgetsbetter.org (for those suffering LGBTQ abuse)*

## Bystanders

The role of bystanders is often ignored in discussions about online bullying, but they can play an important role in encouraging children to take action. Don't forget the famous saying attributed to Edmund Burke: "The only thing necessary for the triumph of evil is that good men do nothing." When a situation is already difficult, the real-time nature of social media can feed the situation, but it can also be used to ease tension and allow friends of the victim to declare themselves as "digital allies". If someone spots a hurtful comment, three others can then come in and protest against the posting. Matthew Bent, whose son was being bullied, took this one step further in March 2013, posting a Facebook photo holding a sign declaring: "I stand behind my son in the fight against bullying!" because he felt that the authorities (the school and the police) hadn't taken him seriously.[35]

The MediaSmarts Report 2012 demonstrated that children in fact show strong resilience when it comes to cyberbullying, having clear strategies in place: "First, ignore it and de-friend or block the person (typically a very successful strategy)." If that doesn't work, they'll seek to confront the bully face to face. If that's not feasible, or doesn't work, they'll call in their parents.

Their research, however, found that most school anti-bullying programmes were a waste of time. The school authorities didn't truly understand the problems being faced, and bringing a teacher into the situations tended to make things worse. Police are often brought into schools to deliver anti-bullying training, but Nancy Willard feels that this is often counter-productive. Most police personnel see only the worst results of bullying behaviour, so tend to over-focus on the negative. The children at highest risk don't tend to trust adults, which adds to their lack of effectiveness. She recommends that the audience for such talks should be digitally more savvy students who already trust adults, understand the bigger picture, and can look out for more "dangerous" behaviour among peers.[36] With this in mind, it's worth looking at "cyber mentor" training, designed for eleven- to seventeen-year-olds, who mentor both offline and online via the BeatBullying website.[37]

*www.cyberbullying.org offers some good advice, worth taking on board at any age:*

- *Learn healthy scepticism: never believe someone is necessarily who they say they are online.*
- *Teach "netiquette": be polite to others online, and don't respond to those seeking a reaction.*
- *Don't send messages when upset: you can't put toothpaste back in the tube.*
- *Don't open messages from someone you don't know.*
- *Trust your instincts.*
- *Don't spend all your time online.*

The least helpful approach is that of "zero tolerance" of the bully, as children need help rather than banishment. The irony is that few educators seem keen to look for an educational approach in which children can learn from their mistakes. If the bully then feels abandoned, and the underlying causes that led to their bullying have not been dealt with, they will make use of the many online opportunities to connect with others who are in tune with how they feel.[38]

### *What if your child is the one doing the bullying?*
No one likes to think that their child is being a bully, but the truth is that there are bullies out there, and your child may be one of them. Factors that have been identified as making a child more likely to become a bully include:
- being a victim of cyberbullying
- not seeing cyberbullying as a problem
- extreme experimentation with different identities
- lack of peer acceptance, or jealousy of peers
- wanting revenge after rejection
- wanting to do something just for the "fun" of it
- needing power or attention
- hating the victim
- being male
- being older
- spending a lot of time online
- being computer-confident
- having a computer in their own room.

Earlier we talked about "disinhibition". With regard to cyberbullying, this is important, as the bully is disconnected from the impact of their bullying (in the same way as, in war, bombers don't see the huge numbers that they kill). The bullies don't see the distress they cause, they feel safe from being caught, and, protected by the technology, they are able to say things they would never say offline. Children will find ways to justify what they are doing that don't fit normal moral standards[39]: they were "just playing around", "someone else told them to", they didn't think the harm caused would be significant, or they dehumanized or blamed the victim. So, if your child is bullying others, talk to them, help them to identify what behaviours count as bullying and to understand the consequences of their actions. Try to understand why they are bullying, and if the answer is as simple as they are bored, look for activities for them to take part in.

For many, it won't be as simple as this. Your child won't necessarily want to sit and listen, and may be actively looking for opportunities to bully once more, waiting until late at night to access the internet, shutting down their devices as soon as you appear. This may be a good time to monitor what your child is doing online, and to restrict their access to technology:

- Remove their internet and mobile privileges (for a fixed period).
- Get them to write an essay on the dangers of cyberbullying.
- Give them a book to read about cyberbullying.
- Assign them community service.
- Encourage them to apologize and take responsibility.

**EXERCISE: Discuss with your child what defines bullying, and how to respond as a target or a bystander, and think about what positive actions can be taken.**

### "Stranger danger" lurks...

Many parents are worried about "stranger danger", something previously confined to spaces outside the house. With mobile devices and computers in many bedrooms, this fear has now entered the home. At the heart of this is a fear of grooming or abduction (which we'll return to later in the book), but parents need to remember that *out of 300,000 child abductions every year, only 12 are by strangers* (US Statistics, 2006).[40] Limiting children's access to online spaces does not help in the long run, as much of our fear of "stranger danger" has been created by years of our society's collective imagination. The media often exaggerate this fear on the basis of a few "cautionary tales", causing disproportionate concerns and reactions. There are risks, but we need to put them into perspective, particularly as there are now so many "good" reasons for meeting strangers, and predators are, thankfully, rare.

In her 2008 review, Professor Byron made the point that the number of incidents of harm from strangers compared to the level of contact is low, as it remains the case that very few abusers of children are strangers to them. It's entirely likely that strangers really are just other children who want to make friends:

> *We must treat the threat of online predators with the seriousness it deserves while at the same time not losing sight of other risks posed to children, both offline and online.*[41]

*"I got a random add from this guy the other day; he was, like, old... I didn't accept him; I was, like, ignore. My mum goes, Who's that? And I go, I haven't a clue, and she goes, Don't you dare add him! And I go, Don't worry, I'm not going to!"*

**CHILDWISE "Digital Lives" 2010, Girls 14 to 15**

Research showed that strangers who attempted to insinuate themselves into "friends only" spaces were suspect and unwelcome. Girls were more likely to break rules about connecting with strangers, fitting in with stereotypes that girls are more into communication. The girls acknowledged the risk of "dirty old men" but felt that they were mature and competent enough to be able to keep themselves safe online through talking to other friends, and, if taking the step to meet up, meeting in public with other friends. Any negative experiences were kept from parents, as they didn't want to worry them and were concerned that restrictions would be placed on their use of the internet. Children noted that sexual innocence was expected by parents, but they thought their parents were naïve in this respect. There was nothing on the internet they hadn't really been able to secure elsewhere via films and magazines, etc.[42]

### Making friends online?

Professor Sonia Livingstone demonstrates how friendships are negotiated through complex networks of relationships as "strangers" become friends, often starting as friends of friends. Members of online communities spend a lot of time together, and "it becomes increasingly difficult to differentiate friends from strangers".[43] Introverts are less likely to meet someone online than extroverts, who "view every stranger as a potential friend", are often confident in communication, spend longer online, and have a wider range of contacts, some of whom are more likely to be strangers. Numbers are small, however, and few of those are complete strangers, as they are often friends of friends. The danger arises when those children who are more vulnerable seek emotional or social compensation from those they meet online. The ones who are harmed by these experiences tend to be younger children, or those who already have psychological difficulties.

The CHILDWISE "Digital Lives" Report 2010 revealed that most children believe that, as long as they don't actually meet the stranger, no harm will come to them. Some have wide-open accounts, while others lock their accounts down. One girl was embarrassed to have refused to webchat with someone and then realized that she (vaguely) knew him, which was likely to make her less cautious with the next person who attempted to connect.

The Oxford Internet Institute research (2011) revealed that despite media concerns about cyberstalking, women had become more likely than men to meet an acquaintance offline whom they had first encountered online, with an increase of 19 per cent prepared to do so. Men's willingness had increased, but not on the same scale.[44] As many parents are increasingly meeting others through online means, there is a sense emerging that it is hypocritical to ban children from doing so. The online sphere offers a space to meet and connect with like-minded people, so parents need to look at putting safe measures in place to make the experience pleasurable. As "Sanya2135", a commentator on an article in the *Washington Post*, put it:

> *Parents must teach their children to safely negotiate a modern world where many people meet and interact online before meeting in person. A blanket "never meet" rule is just astoundingly silly in an age where the parents of these children themselves may well have met online.*[45]

As an eighteen-year-old I spent time in Brazil, and had a great opportunity to stay with a couple whom I'd met on the way over. After the family I was staying with had taken the time to check them out, this was agreed, and it became one of the highlights of the trip.

**EXERCISE: Take time to talk to your child about hopes and fears for online friendships. Establish ground rules for meeting up with a new "friend", including meeting in a public place, being with friends, having a back-up plan, and agreeing not to be left alone with that person.**

CHILDWISE "Digital Lives" 2010 comments:

- "Children in the past were at risk from strangers in the real world – the world is not more wicked, it just has better technology."
- "Online has risks, just as the real world does, but it also has many benefits, in terms of entertainment and education resources."

Sara Batts completed her PhD in 2013, investigating how English Christian groups use the internet. Churches do a lot of work with young people, so safety (online) is a high priority:

> By categorising the Internet as a dangerous place, and only discussing its use within the context of safeguarding, leaders' perceptions of the possibilities of websites may be clouded. A sense of negativity might pervade the discussions if the dangers and not the benefits are highlighted. Studies of young people's use of the Internet have shown that the incidences of unwanted contact *may be over-reported and taken out of context*.[46] (Emphasis added.)

# 9

# Increasingly Mobile

When CHILDWISE undertook their research into children online in 2010, the mobile phone was still not the "channel of choice", because widespread Wi-Fi and suitable contracts didn't exist. A lot has changed since then, and the mobile phone is now the most likely way for many children to connect online, bringing with it a range of concerns for parents, including worries about monitoring use, the challenge of what age to allow your child to have a phone, and what kind of contract to have. A phone provides more freedom to access material online, and is preferred by teenagers who otherwise may have to share a desktop PC with family, with limited time and privacy available.[1]

*Questionnaire respondents were asked what they feared, and what practices they had in place, with regard to digital technology:*

• • • • • • • • • • • • • • • • • • • • • • • • • • • • • • • •

In particular, as my children get more and more access to smartphones or other mobile devices, there is currently very little in the way of tools to enable me to restrict or monitor it, which hugely curtails my ability to parent them responsibly.

**(Parent, 6 to 9, 10 to 12)**

Smartphone use is monitored mainly by bill, and by conversations about usage. I'm considering stronger monitoring following the download of some suspicious apps (identity security reasons rather than other concerns).

**(Parent, 10 to 12)**

The majority of children in the Western world now have a mobile phone, particularly those over the age of eleven, and use them for a mixture of text messaging and making or receiving calls. They are also used for photos, games, video, the internet, music, Bluetooth, downloading apps, social networks, and listening to the radio. In 2012 children were spending around 1.1 hours per day on their mobiles (other than for voice calls). Since 2011, the tablet device (particularly the iPad and the iPad Mini) has also gained significant market share, especially among younger children for whom managing a mouse is hard, but swiping a screen is not. The expectation is that they will be outselling PCs by the end of 2013.[2]

*The world has become increasingly mobile. See this video produced by Erik Qualman, focusing on "mobilenomics": http://www.youtube.com/watch?v=GRiwUCXP08U*

*Some ways in which questionnaire respondents think the mobile has affected their daily lives:*

Helping children to be wise and discerning seems so important as all the checks and locks and safeguards are very hard to administer when they have access to the internet via a smartphone. This is the route we are following at present. It may need to change in the future, but at present it is working well.

**(Parent, 10 to 12)**

> We appreciate the freedom [the mobile phone]
> gives us all to chat at any time and make flexible
> arrangements knowing we can be contacted easily. But
> children have much more personal freedom with it —
> gone are the days of asking your parents if you can
> use the phone to call your boyfriend/girlfriend and
> having to sit in the hall or living room to talk to
> them! Then there is an extra level of intimacy which
> can be reached very early by having phone/text at
> your bedside.
>
> **(Parent, 13 to 15, 16 to 18)**

danah boyd notes that the modern mobile is like a Swiss Army knife – it has lots of potential applications, but we tend to use the same ones over and over again, with more people interested in the options of design and personalization rather than the functions of their phone. Observing the behaviour of many mobile phone users in 2006, she found that 80 per cent never turned it off, while others did so for four to twelve hours in a twenty-four-hour period (usually for sleep, work or the cinema), although many more simply switched to the "vibrate" function. Because of "FOMO" (Fear of Missing Out), mobile-free time is seen as a bit of a luxury enjoyed only by those who feel secure in their position in their social network (and I'm not just talking Facebook here). Thus 80 per cent never turn their phone off, partly to enable friends to be able to get in touch if they are having a bad time. One sixteen-year-old girl, however, said:

*I believe that in order to have a healthy mobile phone culture we need to find out how we can avoid the demand of being publicly present around the clock. To have some clear restrictions when people have time to turn off their mobile, the computer, and log off completely – to prevent stress becoming a national disease.*[3]

The mobile phone has become a part of daily life, acting as a "life log" for many, collecting personal experiences in sound, photo, and video form, "proving" that a user has been somewhere and allowing friends to share their daily activities, although in order to remain part of particular social groups, social codes need to be adhered to.

## An intruder?

Since so many access websites *only* via a mobile, it has become increasingly unacceptable for mobiles to offer a second-rate experience compared to that of the desktop computer. One benefit of the increasing number of mobile devices is that we can exchange a richer variety of information on the move. Previously, if we wanted to use digital technology we were tethered to a screen inside; now we can be out and about and still connected.

Many in danah boyd's research group felt distant from a friend who was on the phone to another person, but liked being able to get hold of that friend if they were the one calling. If bored and lonely at an event people may sit and text other friends, thereby demonstrating that they have other fish to fry. This can have a drawback, as it means people do not need to make an effort to be sociable with those who are physically present. Ozlem Ayduk, an associate professor in the Relationships and Social Cognition Lab at the University of California, Berkeley, says this is not all down to the technology: children sitting at the dinner table with a print book or crayons are not engaged with the people around them either. "There are value-based lessons for children to talk to the people during a meal," she said. "It's not so much about the iPad versus non-electronics."[4]

*Several questionnaire respondents made comments on the rules they have set about appropriate use of mobiles, especially at mealtimes:*

We have open discussions about our day and anything else of interest while at the dinner table every evening.

**(Parent, 16 to 18, 19 or over)**

We also have a strict rule that we don't bring screens to events that are meant to be live events (theatre, concerts, readings). We look down our noses at people who sit at a table together at a restaurant and bury their faces in their screens.

**(Parent, 10 to 12)**

Academics such as Sherry Turkle have raised concerns that because children are economically reliant on their parents for their first phones, their parents expect them to be "on call" at all times. In turn, this means the children become used to turning to their parents first in every situation via the "digital leash".[5] While this sounds great in terms of communication, she fears that children won't develop an ability to be alone and reflect on their own emotions, and will not develop self-sufficiency skills.

## An e-babysitter?

In recent years there has been rapid uptake of smartphones and tablets by children of all ages. CBeebies senior content producer Tim Jokl said: "Last Christmas [2012] seemed like a tipping point for sales of these things", as the website "noticed that suddenly it had quite a few hundred thousand people trying to access the website every week from a tablet".[6]

Access to apps could be useful for entertainment during (e.g.) aeroplane journeys/times when a child is enclosed with little to look at.

**(Parent, 2 or under)**

In 2006, the US-based Kaiser Family Foundation produced an influential report[7] which noted that technology can really help to "keep the peace", "manage schedules", and also act as an "e-babysitter". It's not a term that we have to run away from. Daniel Anderson, Professor of Psychology, at the University of Massachusetts, has studied children's engagement with TV for thirty years. He has noted that children can find it difficult to know where to look when watching TV, but, with the iPad, the action happens where the finger is. With a vocabulary app such as Martha Speaks, there are noticeable gains in vocabulary range. When parents think that a child is "in a trance" on the iPad, they are usually just concentrating (as they may be if deep into reading a book).[8]

*Several questionnaire respondents offered insights into the benefits they see from mobile/touch technology:*

• • • • • • • • • • • • • • • • • • • • • • • • • • • • •

Touch-screen technology is much more intuitive and enables engagement with potentially more complex processes both from an earlier age and also for a wider group of children with differing abilities.
**(Parent, 3 to 5, 10 to 12, 13 to 15, 16 to 18)**

• • • • • • • • • • • • • • • • • • • • • • • • • • • • •

Both are able to play games on my mobile phone. I believe it will help with eye—finger co-ordination and give them a sense of achieving something.
**(Grandmother, 2 and 4)**

• • • • • • • • • • • • • • • • • • • • • • • • • • • • •

My three and a half year old boy loves anything to do with computers and especially likes using iPhones (both mine and my wife's). He can navigate through menus more efficiently and quickly than we can, and understands how to do things without even being able to read. This gives him confidence and freedom of expression; he uses technology to learn — numbers and letters, and skills used in games — finger dexterity and hand—eye co-ordination, for example.

**(Parent, 2 or under, 3 to 5)**

• • • • • • • • • • • • • • • • • • • • • • • • • • • • • • • • • • • • • • •

My little girl could unlock my touch-screen phone before she could walk! She now loves playing on the CBeebies website and the games are really educational and stimulating. She has also started playing Sudoku and chess on phone apps. The main benefits for her at the moment are educational.

**(Parent, 3 to 5)**

Although children are likely to enjoy using the iPad on their own, try to ensure that it is not just a solitary pastime. This can help you understand how your child is using the iPad and provides space to discuss any potential problems. Michaela Wooldridge, a developmental psychologist in western Canada, recently carried out a study to see if the ways mothers interacted with their toddlers differed depending on whether they were playing with traditional toys such as a shape sorter, a book or a toy animal or with battery-powered equivalents. She found that with the electronic toys:

*Parents were not less affectionate, but they were less responsive, less encouraging and did far less teaching. It was almost like the toy was interfering. They were trying to figure out a) how to make it work and b) how to have the child make it work.*[9]

Many parents would justify the use of digital devices solely for learning purposes:

. . . . . . . . . . . . . . . . . . . . . . . . . . . . . . . . . . . . . .

> I think the digital age is moving so fast that it is
> hard to keep up. As a family we believe technology
> is important, but use it only for learning, and for
> the children to play their games (which we restrict
> in relation to time).
>
> **(Parent, 6 to 9)**

An article on *Mashable* noted that educational games for children aged eight to thirteen are largely missing from tablets.[10] There's a lot of emphasis on whether apps are "educational", but what counts as educational, and does everything have to be held up to that standard? Children need "nothing" time, and, yes, "outdoor time", although the increasing portability of computing power (and inventions such as Google Glass) means that the digital can augment "outdoor time" in some circumstances. Parents need to be aware, however, that many iPad/tablet apps are designed to stimulate dopamine release (which affects the brain's rewards and pleasure centres), through offering rewards/exciting visuals at unpredictable times, in order to keep children playing.[11] This is good for the games makers, but dangerously addictive for some users.

*Questionnaire respondents offered insights into how they controlled the use of technology within the family:*

. . . . . . . . . . . . . . . . . . . . . . . . . . . . . . . . . . . . . .

> My younger son has very little unsupervised access,
> in that I control the games he plays on the iPhone
> and iPad. Occasionally I have found him playing
> inappropriate games and watching inappropriate clips
> on YouTube. We have discussed with him why these are
> inappropriate and then "banned" them. On the whole
> he complies with these "bans" but, like any other
> seven-year-old, he likes to push the boundaries.
>
> **(Parent, 6 to 9, 13 to 15)**

> At the moment it is supervised use. They borrow our
> phones and iPads to play games. Only we have the
> passwords to unlock the devices or download new
> games.
>
> **(Parent, 3 to 5, 6 to 9)**

Over 13 billion apps were downloaded in the first three months of 2013.[12] As some parents have found out to their cost (we've all seen the newspaper headlines), although many are free, all require a log in, linked to a credit card, which can allow "in-app" purchases such as extra lives and bonus levels, often at small amounts such as 69p. These soon add up: I got caught out in my first games with *Candy Crush*, and managed to spend about £40 in five hours – needless to say, I have changed my playing habits. Some children and teenagers, however, might not understand that in-app purchases cost real money and parents need to talk to children about that, or ensure that settings prevent this. After a number of parents got caught out with large bills, Apple refunded some costs,[13] and now requires a password to be entered before each purchase. We need to remember, however, that game developers tend not to be altruistic: they have carefully built each game to keep you involved for the longest possible time, and to spend as much as possible.[14]

*You'll probably find that your children get suggestions from their friends, and you get them from other parents, but here are some places to start to find children's apps:*

- *http://www.bestkidsapps.com*
- *http://funeducationalapps.com*
- *http://www.guardian.co.uk/technology/appsblog/2013/ jun/19/50-best-apps-kids-iphone-android-ipad*
- *http://www.guardian.co.uk/technology/2012/aug/04/50-best- apps-chidren-smartphones-tablets*

*To lock down the settings on your phone, see these articles:*

- *iPhone: http://www.guardian.co.uk/technology/appsblog/gallery /2013/apr/17/how-to-stop-children-inapp-purchases-ios*
- *Android: http://www.guardian.co.uk/technology/appsblog/gallery /2013/apr/17/how-to-stop-children-inapp-purchases-android*

## Managing phone use and costs

● ● ● ● ● ● ● ● ● ● ● ● ● ● ● ● ● ● ● ● ● ● ● ● ● ● ● ● ● ● ●

I went with my daughter to the O2 shop to set up an account she would be paying for because she wanted me to help her.

**(Parent, 19+)**

As contracts have become more usable, the number of people possessing phones has grown. BlackBerries are particularly popular with teenagers because of BBM (BlackBerry Messenger), although at the time of writing it was about to become available on iPhones and Android phones.[15] Many parents have refused to buy expensive phones, with questionnaire responses recommending the teenage years as the earliest for a smartphone:

● ● ● ● ● ● ● ● ● ● ● ● ● ● ● ● ● ● ● ● ● ● ● ● ● ● ● ● ● ● ●

Our three children have a mobile. The youngest is nine, but her phone is an old disused handset that is topped up only when she is staying away from home. The other two (thirteen and fifteen) do get hooked into pinging and BBM — phones are often confiscated.

**(Parent, 6 to 9, 13 to 15)**

Many parents buy mobiles for their children because it makes them feel they are always contactable and therefore safer. It is also worth investigating the help given by shops and networks to keep your child safe, including considerations of insurance, age-appropriate settings, content filters, usage controls, location privacy, blocking explicit content, and turning off the ability to buy apps, etc. Don't think about turning the internet off on the phone, otherwise what is the point of a smartphone?

*Each of the networks, and some of the shops, have their own advice for parents/children:*

- *O2: http://www.O2.co.uk/parents (wide range of useful advice, check out: http://www.o2.co.uk/support/generalhelp/howdoi/ safetycontrolandaccess/parentalcontrol)*
- *Vodafone: http://www.vodafone.com/content/index/parents.html (includes the free Digital Parenting magazine)*
- *EE: http://explore.ee.co.uk/digital-living/keeping-children-safe (includes a series of videos explaining core social netiquette)*
- *Three: http://j.mp/three-parent-control (parental control settings)*
- *BlackBerry: http://j.mp/BBM-parents (advice for managing spam, etc.)*
- *PhoneBrain: http://www.phonebrain.org.uk – useful advice for managing the responsibilities of owning a phone (for children, teens, teachers, parents)*
- *Carphone Warehouse: http://www.carphonewarehouse.com/mobile websafety*
- *Phones4u: http://www.phones4u.co.uk/mobile-security?CID=Affiliate _78888*
- *Mumsnet: http://www.mumsnet.com/Internet-safety/mobile-phones*

When shopping for mobile phones, if you're not going for "Pay-as-you-go", look for contract plans that cover both phone calls and data (internet) use, but ask about caps on overspending, and how to block unsuitable sites. Although written in 2006, this checklist: http://kidsmart.org.uk/downloads/mobilesQ. pdf is still very relevant for helping parents to buy a phone, and includes questions regarding Bluetooth, premium-rate numbers, and international roaming (although many operators now have a maximum daily rate abroad). We mentioned in the section "Buy Me! Buy Me!" that parents are coming to terms with how to manage digital pocket money. With regard to mobile phones, an increasing number of children are now on contract deals, including texts and data, spending around £15 per month, with the majority being paid for by their parents.[16]

## At what age should I buy my child a mobile?

*"Mom, everyone has technology but me!" my four-year-old son sometimes wails. And why shouldn't he feel entitled? In the same span of time it took him to learn how to say that sentence, thousands of kids' apps have been developed – the majority aimed at pre-schoolers like him.*[17]

In 2013 the "1stFone" was developed specifically for four-year-olds. With essential functionality only, its maker believes it will reduce the risk of its owner being cyberbullied, sexted or mugged or seeing what they shouldn't online. Parents can enter twelve numbers into the memory, along with an entry for 999, and the child won't be able to call anyone else. Comments in newspaper articles demonstrated that some parents thought that it was wrong to be marketing to four-year-olds at all or that they shouldn't be left in a situation where a phone might be required, whereas others believed that it was good for emergencies, and would introduce children to basic phone knowledge.[18] At the other end of the scale, there are phones described as being for "seniors", which tend to have large buttons, simple, non-confusing functionality, and SOS buttons. Why not get your children to help the seniors they know with their phones, according to the expertise of each?

Research shows that, on average, children receive their first mobile at the age of eight. Other parents see secondary school as a more appropriate point, as at this stage children are more likely to travel, partake in after-school activities independently, and visit friends. For separated or divorced parents whose children don't live with them all the time, mobiles can be a very useful way of staying in touch. In any case, all parents should research and make their own decisions, rather than give in to pester power.[19]

*Questionnaire respondents were asked if they would place age limits on particular technologies:*

• • • • • • • • • • • • • • • • • • • • • • • • • • • • • • • • • • •

Kids have to show they are trustworthy on a desktop under supervision before being given use of a low-end and low-contract smartphone or other such gadget. This means that there is a scale of "upgradability" depending on how appropriately it is used. The age at which that rule is applicable will vary from child to child.

**(Parent, 16 to 18)**

• • • • • • • • • • • • • • • • • • • • • • • • • • • • • • • • • • •

We provided only basic phones and minimum contracts — if they wanted a smartphone they had to save up and get their own. This happened when they were responsible enough to hold down their first jobs at fourteen to sixteen.

**(Parent, 16 to 18, 19 or over)**

• • • • • • • • • • • • • • • • • • • • • • • • • • • • • • • • • • •

I have also said no to a mobile at present, although we will reconsider when he goes to secondary school at eleven so that he can contact us if necessary, e.g. when he misses the school bus. I would not necessarily let him have a smartphone, though. I haven't got one, so why should he?!

**(Parent, 6 to 9)**

• • • • • • • • • • • • • • • • • • • • • • • • • • • • • • • • • • •

Our children have to get the bus to school from our village from the age of nine so we allow them mobile

phones then, but only basic, cheap ones. My daughter
was thirteen when she got her first smartphone and I
would imagine the boys will be the same.

**(Parent, 3 to 5, 6 to 9, 13 to 15)**

Typical questionnaire answers stated that children don't really
need a phone until secondary school, although if there is a
spare, old device, it might be passed on. There was a feeling that
smartphones aren't required until at least the age of thirteen,
and are more likely to be needed around GCSE time:

• • • • • • • • • • • • • • • • • • • • • • • • • • • • • • • • • •

We won't be buying our daughters mobile phones until
they go to secondary school, and then they will
be cheap, basic ones, because they might get lost
or stolen, and they could waste too much time — or
money — using a smartphone.

**(Parent, 6 to 9, 10 to 12)**

An ideal time to discuss mobile phone boundaries with your
child is the day you buy their first one. These should include:

- sticking to a budget
- understanding what to do about security if the phone gets
  stolen
- limiting the chances of it being stolen
- knowing what will happen if they lose or break it.

If the child of one of my friends leaves their mobile carelessly
lying around, or leaves it behind at an event, they lose the use
of it for the length of time it would have taken to replace it,
in order to teach them responsibility. You could even go as far
as Janell Hofmann, who gave her son an iPhone but with a
"contract", which finishes with: "You will mess up. I will take
away your phone. We will sit down and talk about it. We will
start over again."[20]

## Texting and short forms

Texting is an efficient short form of communication that allows a conversation to continue over time, without a commitment to respond immediately. *Wired* Magazine interviewed children, some of who said that phone conversations made them anxious: they didn't want others to overhear their conversations, and worried if there was no response and that mobile calls drained the batteries. They noted that young people are made anxious by a lack of response, a fear that the message has been misunderstood, and the belief that they've not been invited to the "cool" parties[21] – although that fear is as old as time itself.

It's helpful to understand the texting habits of children and youth today. Statistics are bandied about with regard to text use by teenagers, with Edgington describing any of those sending over 120 text messages per day as hyper-texters, with a tendency to exhibit other bingeing or promiscuous behaviour and to be susceptible to peer pressure.[22] If your child is sending over 3,600 texts a month it may be time to talk to them, although with so many unlimited text packages, which are otherwise recommended, it can be hard to tell. Interviewed for *The Guardian,* Philippa reckoned she sent "probably about thirty" text messages every day and received as many. Most are about meeting up or discussing homework, or, particularly, are triggered by boredom. She wouldn't dream of using her phone to actually phone anyone, except perhaps to placate her parents or ask them to pick her up. Calls are expensive, and can't be made in the classroom – where many text, although they know that they shouldn't.[23]

As the younger generations increasingly use textspeak, we have to recognize that they can't conform to the same standard of literacy that we learned. Tracy Rolling, a user experience specialist for Nokia, noted in 2012 that we've had fears for the last fifteen years that text messaging will damage children's literacy:

*It turns out that kids who use (and invent) text-message shorthand have better verbal skills than us oldsters do because text-message shorthand is inventive word play. The kids aren't smarter or dumber than we were; technology helps us free our brains for more useful things.*[24]

### A few common examples of textspeak:

- *ACORN: Really nutty person*
- *ASL: Age, sex, location*
- *BFF: Best friends forever*
- *GAL: Get a life*
- *GSOH: Good sense of humour*
- *HMU: Hit me up*
- *IDK: I don't know*
- *IRL: In real life*
- *LOL: Laugh out loud*
- *LMIRL: Let's meet in real life*
- *NBD: No big deal*
- *PRW: Parents are watching*
- *ROFL: Rolling on the floor laughing*
- *10Q: Thank you*
- *TISNF: That is so not fair*
- *TMI: Too much information*
- *TBH: To be honest*
- *WRU: Where are you?*

### Where to look for more:

- *http://www.netlingo.co/acronyms.php*
- *http://www.webopedia.com/quick_ref/ textmessageabbreviations.asp*
- *http://computersavvy.wordpress.com/2009/06/03/text-message-and-chat-room-short-form-dictionary-letters-a-z-ver-2–0/*
- *http://www.urbandictionary.com*

# 10

# Sex Talk
# (Porn, Paedophilia, and Sexting)

· · · · · · · · · · · · · · · · · · · · · · · · · · · · · · · · ·

As a foster carer I have witnessed children being exposed to inappropriate content from the web, DVDs, and Xbox and PlayStation games. There is plenty of evidence to demonstrate that exposure to sexual scenes and violence can negatively influence the behaviour of children – our next generation. Unfortunately we cannot rely on good parenting by some. Are we not a society that protects and supports the more vulnerable? Why therefore are we neglecting our children?

**(Carer, 6 to 9, 10 to 12)**

These are fairly familiar fears for all who have responsibility for children, and it is important to be aware of the more vulnerable among them. With regard to your own children, ensure that they don't become "vulnerable users", bereft of supportive and communicative parents. As with any problem online, if children encounter sexual content, they should:

- STOP: don't react
- SAVE: what they're doing
- SHARE: the information with an adult they trust.

Professor Sonia Livingstone highlights the fact that although there is a risk of having negative experiences online, those with psychological difficulties are more likely to experience intense or longer-lasting harm. Those who are resilient offline are more likely to adapt well online, whereas those vulnerable offline are also more vulnerable online.[1] MediaSmarts research from 2012 offers encouragement in that most of those they surveyed were well aware of the online risks, managed their own behaviour to avoid them, demonstrated resilience when encountering them, and actively sought out parental guidance when needed.

## Porn

The media have focused heavily on the "dangers of porn" online for children, to the extent that many parents feel they are powerless to stop it. Professor Livingstone adds that debate in this area can be difficult, as the media tend to mix up a range of complex issues into one big scare story. The EU Kids Online survey demonstrated that only 6,000 of the 25,000 children surveyed had encountered even a single sexual image online;[2] still a high number but not every child, in contrast to the media impression.

• • • • • • • • • • • • • • • • • • • • • • • • • • • • • • • • • • •

We talk fairly openly about pornography and gambling and the negative effect they can have on our lives, and about how much better it is to encourage and support others rather than abusing our power and putting people down. I have joined several lobby groups that try to make adult content a "sign-in" feature for adults only, to make it harder to access

and download, and to help prevent young children being accidentally exposed to pornographic images.
**(Parent, 16 to 18, 19 or over)**

The tendency for young people to search for adult material of a sexual nature has been common for years; in many ways it's a "rite of passage". The core difference is that until recently it took some effort to acquire printed pornographic material, whereas huge amounts circulate freely online, much of it more hard-core and violent in nature than before. Those who deliberately seek this material out online tend to know how to delete their internet history and cookies, so parents may not be aware or may think that *their* child surely couldn't be into such things. The EU Kids Online survey demonstrated that, because it's so easily available online, many think that it is fine: no one can see them and they are sure that they won't get caught.

The EU Kids Online survey also showed that boys were more likely to seek out pornographic content, or to be sent links to it, while girls appeared to feel more upset by what they saw and, in particular, became concerned about sexual expectations for their own future. Dr Heather Wood from an NHS clinic for compulsive sexual behaviour noted that, for young people, there are particular dangers associated with looking at internet pornography:

> *While it is appropriate for a 15-year-old boy to be sexually interested in someone of his own age, a sexual image of a 15-year-old is illegal, and it is a criminal act to download or distribute such an image in the UK.*[3]

Teenage boys may be less interested in those outside their own age group but they are potentially unable to tell the difference between a fourteen-year-old and an eighteen-year-old, so face a higher risk of prosecution if caught accessing images of those of their own age.

In 2010, a Home Office report warned that the "drip-drip" exposure to sexual imagery – including pornography, "lads' mags", and sexual imagery in advertising – was distorting young people's perceptions of themselves; it was "encouraging boys to become fixated on being macho and dominant, and girls to present themselves as sexually available and permissive".[4] Too much emphasis in porn on "the perfect body" is leaving young people unhappy when their own bodies don't match up.[5]

Professor Livingstone, however, points out that children often challenge the representations seen online,[6] and famous blogger "Belle de Jour" would argue that to "help them understand pornography as entertainment, as opposed to how sex should be, we need to stop skipping the subject of real sex and real relationships when talking to young people".[7] As Livingstone's research demonstrates, pornography doesn't exist in a social vacuum: in Western cultures where men and women are purportedly treated as social equals, and assault and harassment are seen as wrong, some citizens of all ages are likely to challenge the existence of pornography as a given.[8]

In the early 2000s, as worries about young people accessing pornography rose, filtering software was proposed as the solution. The arguments continue:

*If car manufacturers had no responsibility for safety measures – i.e. car seats for children, airbags, seat belts – and it was entirely up to parents if they chose to use these, there would be an outcry. So what is the difference with social networking sites? We know the dangers; we know there are negligent parents. We have to protect the children whose parents can't or won't.*[9]

Tom Wood, a sixteen-year-old schoolboy, broke into Australia's $84-million internet porn filter in less than thirty minutes,[10] and as a result recommended that the focus for child internet safety be elsewhere: on educating children to protect themselves and their privacy. Filtering software is valuable for younger children, but we have to expect that older children will try to get around the protection, so don't expect that you can install it and your job is done. Take time to understand how, when and where your children are accessing the internet, and how to deal with distressing material when they come across it. As Sally Peck wrote in *The Telegraph*: "No matter how hard you try, you will not be able to police your child's exposure to everything vile until he is 30."[11]

This is all part of the ongoing debate we referred to earlier about whether the default setting for the internet should be "opt-in" for porn, rather than "opt-out" filtering, something that Mumsnet moved away from after feedback from their more technologically savvy users.[12]

As the NAS report "Youth, Pornography and the Internet" stated:

*Swimming pools can be dangerous for children. To protect them, one can install locks, put up fences, and deploy pool alarms. All of these measures are helpful, but by far the most important thing that one can do for one's children is to teach them to swim.*[13]

Tanya Byron used a similar analogy in 2008: so many adults can only dabble in the shallow end, if in the water at all, and despite the fact that children are very capable they are constantly warned that it is dangerous, and kept away from the pool that is the internet. Rather than leaving them to "drown" in an addiction to porn, parents need to open the conversational gates, however difficult that may be. So parents should take note of the advice given in this questionnaire response:

I think the digital tools that kids have
available now are fantastic if used sensibly
and in conjunction with parental instruction
and supervision. The dangers can be addressed,
especially in younger children, if parents take the
time to acquaint themselves with what their children
are using. Like anything, however, if you leave them
to their own devices they can get into trouble with
these things, and it is up to us as parents to make
them aware of the dangers and equip them to operate
in an online environment safely.

**(Parent, 3 to 5, 6 to 9, 13 to 15)**

## Grooming and child abuse

Earlier on in the book, I mentioned Dan Gardner and his research on fear and risk. He refers to the website of Innocents in Danger, a Swiss-based NGO, which headlines with "Some Terrifying Statistics", and then states: "Recent figures suggest some fifty thousand paedophiles are prowling the internet at any one time." There's no source given for the claim. This statistic is given repeatedly in speeches and headlines, but it is a suspicious number: it's so round, and so easy to pluck out of the air. It's also a figure that's actually impossible to collect, because people aren't going to declare themselves to be a paedophile in surveys. Those who produce monitoring software such as SpectorSoft™ are keen to use these statistics to scare parents, and says these paedophiles have "one goal in mind: to find a child, strike up a relationship and eventually meet the child". The number of 50,000 has appeared in relation to two previous panics: the number of children kidnapped by strangers in the early 1980s and the number of murders by satanic cults in the late 1980s. Dan Gardner states that although you may realize that the numbers are overblown, the "anchoring rule" ensures that your gut instinct will still feel that it's a big problem – maybe 10,000 – and therefore it is worth spending money on software to protect your child in this area. As software marketers use this in their advertising, others, including child-protection activists, NGOs, police officers, politicians, and journalists, echo the statistics in support of "the cause".[14]

Witnessing cruelty to animals online affects a much larger number of children than paedophilia and grooming,[15] but the spectre of abduction is the most terrifying prospect that exists for parents. In the Sexual Offences Act of 2003 the law relating to grooming (which existed long before the internet, but, as with other online issues, has increased in speed and scope) was changed to become pre-emptive (not waiting for abuse to be confirmed) rather than reactive, to increase the chances of preventing child sexual abuse. The Child Exploitation and Online Protection Centre (CEOP) in the UK noted that the number reporting abuse was around 1,000 per month in early 2012.[16] At least a quarter of these were suspected grooming cases, rather than cases where there was actual evidence. There was also some suspicion that a number of people were testing out the button. Statistically, road safety is still a bigger problem, but awareness of grooming has grown.

Online sexual grooming occurs when someone makes contact with a child with the motive of preparing them for sexual abuse, either online or offline. So what are you looking out for? When reading the list below, remember that none of these in isolation means that grooming is actually taking place. As we pointed out in "Friendships", many of these will come from children genuinely seeking friendship:

- gathering personal details, such as age, name, address, mobile number, name of school, and photographs
- offering opportunities for modelling, particularly to young girls
- promising meetings with pop idols or celebrities, or offers of merchandise
- offering cheap tickets to sporting or music events

- offering material gifts, including electronic games, music or software
- offering virtual gifts, such as rewards, passwords, and gaming cheats
- suggesting quick and easy ways to make money
- paying young people to appear naked and perform sexual acts via webcams
- gaining a child's confidence by offering positive attention
- encouraging the child to share or talk about any difficulties or problems at home
- providing a sympathetic and supportive response
- bullying and intimidating behaviour, such as threatening to expose the child by contacting their parents to inform them of their child's communications or postings on a social networking site
- saying they know where the child lives or goes to school
- using webcams to spy and take photographs and movies of victims
- asking sexually themed questions, such as "Do you have a boyfriend?" or "Are you a virgin?"
- asking children and young people to meet offline
- sending sexually themed images to a child, depicting adult content or the abuse of other children
- masquerading as a minor or assuming a false identity to deceive a child, using school or hobby sites to gather information about a child's interests, likes, and dislikes.[17]

If you're wondering what the social networks do to protect your children, sites such as Club Penguin have over 200 moderators,[18] while Facebook actively blocks convicted sex offenders from the site, although of course there's no way they can promise 100 per cent success in this. In July 2013 a number of "internet giants" including Facebook, Microsoft, Google, Twitter, and at least three other major companies completed nine months of discussions on plans to wipe out child abuse images from major platforms, which had previously not been possible.[19]

It's also encouraging to know that the police seek to catch paedophiles,[20] and that 97 per cent of children who go missing are found. Social media, indeed, can be used in campaigns to get children back,[21] and you could use a tool such as Wootch on your smartphone, which triggers an alarm if your child wanders more than five metres away.[22]

### *Sources of further information:*

- *https://www.thinkuknow.co.uk/parents/*
- *https://www.facebook.com/note.php?note_id=196124227075034*
- *http://www.google.co.uk/goodtoknow/familysafety/abuse/*
- *http://www.clubpenguinwiki.info/wiki/Report_a_Player*
- *http://www.moshimonsters.com/parents*
- *https://www.iwf.org.uk*

*Questionnaire respondents were asked what steps they take in their own households to ensure the safe use of digital technology:*

• • • • • • • • • • • • • • • • • • • • • • • • • • • • • • • • • • •

Family agreement; discussions of stories in the press where kids have been taken advantage of; main computer is downstairs in a central location (we walk in and out); all passwords are known by us and we occasionally audit content. I'd worry if I thought they were trying to hide something.

**(Parent, 10 to 12, 13 to 15)**

• • • • • • • • • • • • • • • • • • • • • • • • • • • • • • • • • • •

We used explaining and chatting — and pointing out news items to educate them about the risks. That works better than nagging.

**(Parent, 19 or over)**

**EXERCISE: Identify stories about grooming from the press, and get children to discuss how they might have behaved differently, and to think about possible conclusions "if" different choices had been made.**

## Sexting

A widely used definition of sexting is: "The act of sending sexually explicit messages or images, primarily between mobile phones." With easy access to mobile technology, images can spread rapidly, with emotional, social, and criminal consequences. Those who send these messages probably want desperately to fit in, to "prove" they are ready for a relationship, and, being impulsive, don't consider the consequences of their behaviour. As we have seen, the development of apps such as Snapchat has given the illusion of control, as the image "disappears" after a few seconds, but children must understand that copies of it could be made, and are stored on servers on the way through. Parents certainly shouldn't wait for something to happen before talking about this subject – leaving it till later could prove far more embarrassing.

Professor Livingstone noted that it can be difficult to set the boundary between the "fun" and the "coercive", as so much teenage talk is full of sexual innuendo, rude jokes, and swearing.[23] The EU Kids Online research showed that around 15 per cent had seen or received sexts in the previous twelve months, although only 6 per cent of parents thought that their children had seen such messages. There was evidence of greater occurrence in Romania, Estonia, and Poland, all countries where national and familial protection for children is less developed but internet access in the home has grown. Few of those who saw sexting images found them harmful or upsetting, with girls turning to their friends and boys to their technology or simply shrugging their shoulders. Those who *are* upset are usually pre-teenage children, and they may require social and psychological support to understand why they have got involved in an unhealthy relationship, even if that relationship has gone no further than exchanging phone numbers.

There is increasing social pressure to provide sexts, but in many ways it is simply the technological development of that old chestnut "If you loved me, you'd sleep with me". Threats are made that relationships will be broken off if photos are not provided, or previous photos will be sent on to others if the subject doesn't have sex with the recipient of the original sext. Many young people have come to accept sexting as part of life, but it's illegal and constitutes child abuse.[24] If you have instituted regular opportunities to talk about "the digital", then ensure that this is one of the topics covered. If you discover that your child has been involved, talk to them to find out why they do it,[25] seek to understand their motivations, and help them to avoid criminal conviction.[26] Some teenagers, however, are actively looking for sexual hook-ups online and will require a different conversation, and there are also legitimate concerns to be addressed by those over sixteen in relationships with those under sixteen.

The biggest danger point for sexted photos comes at the point of a relationship breakup, when photos may be shared in revenge. For every photo shared, work on the assumption that there is a good possibility it will not remain private. Once out in the public domain, it can quickly multiply and never be taken back. If you receive a sexting image, you should remove it quickly. Police can check, and can follow the data trail in search of "proof" as to what you did with the image. Common sense law then typically applies, otherwise criminal charges, including having to register as a sex offender, can stick for the rest of your life.

It can be particularly difficult for youngsters in an abusive relationship to get out of it, and we all need to be alert to be able to offer support to escape. Abusive relationships can include excessive texting demanding to know where you are and who you are with, sexual demands, blackmail re nude photos, demanding passwords for accounts, and defining whom friendships can be established with. As with cyberbullying, children need to understand that not "everyone is doing this", which could be highlighted via a survey of their peers. MediaSmarts research from 2012 highlighted that within peer groups there is pressure on girls *not* to partake in the sharing of sexualized images – girls were taking extra steps not to be labelled as a "slut", blaming those who had shared such images for their own indiscretion – whereas boys are largely free to do what they like.

With regard to those children who have already shared sexting images, bear in mind they won't be the first or the last to share such photos, and acknowledge that you may not be able to retrieve all images. Assure your child that everyone makes mistakes, and help them deal with the consequences. If possible, get images removed from sites (through contacting service providers), but understand it may not be possible to remove all copies. As photos may have made their way around schools, get the schools involved to limit harassment. Increased awareness campaigns within schools have been having a demonstrable impact, but mostly among the more self-confident, so other policies are needed to deal with the more vulnerable.

# 11

# Keeping within the Law

We have seen in the previous section that legal issues arise online. In general, it is good to assume that the internet is not the Wild West, and to understand that the laws of the land from which you are accessing the internet generally apply within the online spaces, while recognizing the internet's global nature. Online behaviour is "human nature amplified": the crimes that exist offline also exist online, where parents (as offline) are legally responsible and liable for their children's actions.

We have already seen that many sexual images constitute illegal content, as do extreme violent and racist materials, and other illegal online activities include grooming (as we have seen), identity theft, intentionally inflicting emotional distress, invasion of privacy, fraud, and harassment. Southwark Council took out an injunction against "gang member" Matt, believing that YouTube had become a "new playground" for gang members. "By all means we want people to use social media, but we do not want you to use it in ways that will incite violence," said Jonathan Toy, Southwark Council's head of community safety.[1] The legal system tries to make existing laws fit the crimes, but, as technology changes so fast, a number of them need rethinking. At present, however, they stand.

## Plagiarism and copyright

Copyright is a complicated subject, but one that we need to be aware of. I've been to a couple of day courses on it, at which the general advice was "None of this constitutes legal advice; talk to a lawyer". Ryan Cordell, a historian whose children got 1 million "Likes" on Facebook, spoke of how publishers are seeking to "manage" the way that their information is shared in the digital era, echoing the struggles that journalists had in the nineteenth century before systems were formalized.[2]

I have observed many students using music and images from a range of sources and not seeing this as a use of someone else's property, or worrying about questions of ownership. Many students think that copyright law will be applied in the same way that plagiarism rules are applied in school: it is fine to use the material as long as you cite where you've sourced it from. They see this as a compliment to the artist who produced the material. Some producers of material would agree with them, but current copyright law means that this is incorrect. The parents of children using any copyrighted material in digital productions, including music, video, and images, could face criminal proceedings from companies keen to protect their intellectual property.

*Copyright rules have been developed, and you can find the current ones here: http://www.ipo.gov.uk/types/copy.htm*

In recent years, a growing number of users keen to capitalize on the spirit of the World Wide Web (which was "given away" by Tim Berners-Lee for the public good) have created what are known as "Creative Commons" licences, which allow creators to give the public permission to share and use creative work. Six different licences exist, at the heart of which all users must acknowledge the creator as the originator of the work. Creators can choose whether others can share, edit, or make money from the works.[3]

The internet does offer all users a huge library at their fingertips, produced in a range of media, and enabling conversation and collaboration with friends and teachers in the production of homework for schools. There is a temptation for students to simply cut and paste and pretend that it is their own work. Plagiarism research conducted at the University of Winchester showed that, alongside the expertise of lecturers in spotting inconsistencies in writing style, there is an increasing use of software such as Turnitin® that detects material ripped from the internet, or copied from other essays. The Learning and Teaching Team encouraged the use of such software to help students understand what constituted plagiarism, rather than as punishment. Students do, however, need to understand that they can lose their university place (and the fees they have already paid) if they repeatedly plagiarize.

I have always encouraged students to use the internet, but to use it well: to reference what they find, cross-reference it, and dig deeper than the first site they see; to start with Wikipedia, but not to think they can ever finish there.

## Music, film and apps

You may have noticed stores such as HMV disappearing from the high street as downloading has become "the norm", with most children now owning MP3 devices: there were over 1 billion downloads in 2012.[4] The CHILDWISE Monitor Report 2012 found that up to half of all children were watching illegally downloaded movies, usually before they were out in the cinema.

It must be noted that sharing files across computers (known as peer-to-peer file sharing) is illegal, and brings with it an increased danger of viruses, Trojans and spyware as well as prosecution. All downloads should be run through antivirus software such as McAfee or AVG to limit the risk, although it's not entirely eliminated (so good back-up practices are also important). Some don't see why they should pay for something that's available free, but others see paid-for as more dependable, with less risk of viruses, while others recognize that in doing so they are supporting the creators and artists. CHILDWISE anticipated that the wider use of prepaid cards is expected to encourage more legal downloads, and had already noted a rise in the use of legal sites over the last four to five years.

Around a third of children find out about new apps from their friends (particularly girls), and research has shown that boys are generally more willing to pay for apps than girls are. Parents should take note of the "Three strikes rule": warnings about illegal downloads could be sent to parents, who could then be taken to court on the third strike.[5] Children, of course, will also watch their parents' behaviour, so parents need to model good ethical and moral behaviour both online and offline. Otherwise, children will do what you do rather than what you say, and assume it's OK "because I can", and because "everyone does it": I think we had the same debate about cassette tapes! There is no point in saying to children "Don't do this; you will get caught and punished," because they know the odds are extremely low (despite a few high-profile cases), so the message doesn't work. Instead, have conversations about values, and the fact that those making new films or music need money to do it.

### Legitimate sources for downloads:

- *http://www.childnet.com/resources/downloading/home/*
- *http://www.findanyfilm.com (legal film downloads)*
- *http://pro-music.org (legal downloads)*
- *http://www.thecontentmap.com (lists of legal sites)*
- *iTunes: https://itunes.apple.com (music and app downloads)*
- *DoubleTwist: http://www.doubletwist.com (Android equivalent to iTunes)*
- *Tunechecker http://www.tunechecker.com (provided by www.moneysavingexpert.com)*

## Viruses

One of the most common bad experiences for those using the internet is receiving a computer virus. Malware can take over your computer: it can destroy the data on it, cause it to run too slowly, or share files on your computer with hackers, including personal contacts and bank details. As expensive mobile phones get more sophisticated, and because they are always on, it's worth being aware of what you can do to protect these as well.

Here are some basic tips to protect you and your family from viruses and worse:

- Ensure that your devices are protected by passwords and pin codes.
- Install antivirus software. I have the free version from AVG on my laptop and my phone, which also offers anti-theft protection.[6]
- Never open a file sent via email, text or social media message unless it's clear that it's legitimate, or you have checked with the sender what it is.
- Back up your files frequently, either in "the cloud" or on an external hard drive.
- Research apps that you are going to download before downloading, to see what experiences others have had and whether they are reputable.
- Beware of using unsecured Wi-Fi in coffee shops, etc. for any of your services that require passwords, especially banking passwords.
- Make a note of your International Mobile Equipment Identity (IMEI) in case your phone is stolen.
- If you sell on one of your electronic devices, ensure that all the data is removed by restoring the device to its factory settings (if you're not sure how to do it, simply Google "Restore factory settings", preferably with the name of your phone).

# 12

# Health Works

With each new form of technology that significantly alters the way we work (and play), concerns are raised, of both a physical and a psychological nature. We'll have a look at some of those here, including setting up your working area appropriately, accessing "dodgy" health information online, the question of brain changes, addiction, conversational ability, and ensuring there's time for physical fitness in among all the screen time.

## Physical set-up

*Questions to ask about the set-up of your computer area:*

*Chair:*
- *Are you sitting well back in the chair?*
- *Is the backrest properly adjusted to support your back?*
- *Is your seat big enough to support your hips and thighs?*
- *Are your feet well supported on the floor or on a footrest?*
- *Can you rest your arms comfortably on the armrests (if you have them)?*
- *Can you pull right up to your desk or keyboard without hitting your armrests?*

*Keyboard/Pointing device:*
- *Can you reach the keyboard easily?*
- *Is your pointing device within easy reach of you and the keyboard?*
- *Is the most frequently used section of the keyboard positioned directly in front of you?*
- *Have you investigated ergodynamic keyboards and mice?*

*Computer screen/Documents:*
- *Are you sitting directly in front of your screen (not off to one side)?*
- *Can you view the monitor without seeing glare on the screen?*
- *Can you view the screen using a slight downward gaze without raising or lowering your chin?*
- *Is the screen at least an arm's length away from you?*
- *Are any documents you are using on a stand between the monitor and keyboard, or on a stand close to the monitor?*

The main physical concerns include posture at the computer working desk, vision problems from spending too much time looking at a screen, and potential brain damage, so let's deal briefly with each of these in turn. The most important thing is to check the guidance above and ensure that the desk is set up appropriately, also recognizing that every user should get up and stretch on a regular basis.

With regard to vision problems, excessive eye strain is possible if too much time is spent on screen, so frequent breaks should be taken.[1] Some call this the "20–20–10" rule: every twenty minutes users should take their eyes off the computer and look at an object at least twenty feet (six metres) away for at least ten seconds, and the younger the user, the less time you are likely to want them to spend on screen. Ensure that there is backlighting for any screens, and that users are not in a darkened room. Sanford ophthalmologist Dr Geoffrey Tufty said: "When you're concentrating on a near object, such as an iPad or book or iPhone, you blink less. When you blink less, your eyes dry out. When the eyes dry out, they get tired and burn."

If your child is suffering from eye fatigue, Tufty suggests you get them to take a break from the iPad around every fifteen minutes. "Shut it off. Do something that requires them not to focus within that arm's length range." Nevertheless, he says there's no evidence that using tablets or even smartphones can lead to long-term vision problems, and don't forget that they *are* a great learning tool.[2]

No link between brain cancer and mobile phone use has yet been proved, but further research continues – so, in the meantime, prioritize texts over calls, keep calls short and use hands-free so the phone is further from your body.

> **EXERCISE: Take time to look at your computer spaces and implement the advice above. Make a family pact to follow the 20–20–10 rule.**

### Dodgy health information

We all understand that teenagers may not want to speak to parents, teachers, and sometimes even their friends about what is going on in their minds and bodies, and thus search elsewhere for the information they require. This used to come through magazines, books or TV programmes, but with the web at their fingertips virtually all the time, this will be their first point of reference for difficult or embarrassing questions. It's there when they need it, and they can see that others have similar problems, which makes them feel less isolated. However, information on an NHS website indicates how this can become problematic:

> *A fifteen-year-old girl tries to diet but finds herself bingeing soon afterwards. Ashamed, and even more concerned about how this will affect her weight, she searches for help online,*

*but finds a "pro-mia" website. Or a fifty-three-year-old man,
faced with redundancy, wonders how he will manage without
his work and income. Too ashamed to talk to his wife or his
GP, he enters a forum for those suffering from depression,
but instead of support, he finds aggressive interactions and
accounts of self-harm.[3]*

A pro-mia website is one on which those suffering from bulimia
reject the idea that they are ill, and instead exchange tips on
how to be a better bulimic. Recently there has been a growth in
such websites, which allow users to express their feelings and
share information about eating disorders, dieting and body
image, depression, drug and alcohol misuse, sexual infections,
isolation and loneliness, bullying, self-harm, and suicide. This
can be a supportive environment, but often includes negative
elements such as the obvious promotion or encouragement of
self-harm, including filming and publishing these activities.

Dr Rachel O'Connell, an internet safety expert in this area,
notes that many organizations have been reluctant to set up
online health sites, so other sites have grown to fill the gap.
There is a significant danger that, because many sites are
unmoderated, information isn't monitored, so incorrect answers
go unchallenged. In 2012, 10 per cent of European children
aged between eleven and sixteen reported that they had seen
pro-anorexia sites, and this increased to one in five teenage girls
in the fourteen- to sixteen age group. Seven per cent of young
people have seen sites that advocate self-harm and 5 per cent
have seen suicide sites.[4] Don't assume that what your children
are accessing is harmful or that they are intending to act on
what they read in those visits, but look for opportunities to
open discussion about the advice they are looking at.

Reg Bailey's review of the sexualization of young people called
for internet service providers to block access to websites that
encourage harmful behaviour, but Byron's 2010 review expressed

concern that this risked driving vulnerable young people to more obscure sites with more dangerous contacts, adding to any stigma attached to harmful behaviour, and even making harmful behaviour seem more attractive to some. Keeping such information, discussions, and visits in the public arena enables organizations to signpost more appropriate support, and enables collection of data to develop stronger policies and online resources to meet the needs of vulnerable young people.

One area that needs particular monitoring by parents is that of young daughters who want to post photos of themselves online. These are carefully chosen by teenage girls to show the thinnest images (and they sometimes resort to Photoshop). They then use their phones to constantly check their appearance with "selfies", and seek positive feedback on Facebook about each image posted. Teenage girls noticeably comment incessantly on each other's appearance, using such remarks to measure their friendships, self-image, and basic self-worth. Parents should aim to bring such topics into the open, and ensure that children are not left to define their worth by their appearance. During adolescence, this can be a tricky one, because adolescents typically care more about what their peers think than what their parents say, so can you find someone "cooler" whom they will listen to, such as an older sibling or an aunt, or encourage the leader of groups they participate in to open up a group conversation?

### *Some valuable sites to bookmark:*
- *http://getconnected.org.uk (directory of sites)*
- *http://embarrassingbodieskids.channe14.com*
- *http://www.bigwhitewall.com/*
- *http://www.b-eat.co.uk*
- *http://www.youngminds.org.uk*
- *http://www.childline.org.uk/explore/Pages/Explore.aspx*
- *http://youthaccess.org.uk*

- *http://camh.org.uk*
- *http://www.nhs.uk/nhsdirect/Pages/Symptoms.aspx*
- *Find a therapist: http://www.itsgoodtotalk.org.uk/therapists/; http://www.newsavoydirectory.org*

## Brain change?

There are constant references in the media to the "fact" that digital media are "rewiring children's brains". Journalist Nicholas Carr's book *The Shallows* has been particularly influential in this context. He discusses changes in the brain, and how, as a child, he used to get lost in the twists and turns of a book, but now "can't concentrate" as he clicks among the data his brain has become hungry for. As his old computer turned him into a word processor, so the new machine has made him into a high-speed data-processing machine.[5] Technology certainly does make it possible for us to change our practices, but I am a notorious "polymath", and a good book or film, or even (dare I say) the writing process, can draw me in for several hours, so I'm not convinced by his arguments.

Newspaper headlines have promoted the idea that the internet is changing our brains, typically for the worse. In the Pew 2012 "Hyper-connected" survey, a number of experts highlighted how every activity we undertake will affect our brain functioning or our thinking, but that doesn't make it inherently bad. Communications consultant Stowe Boyd said:

*The reason that kids are adapting so quickly to social tools online is because they align directly with human social connection, much of which takes place below our awareness. Social tools are being adopted because they match the shape of our minds, but yes, they also stretch our minds based on use and mastery, just like martial arts, playing the piano, and badminton.*

Blogger, journalist, and communications professor Jeff Jarvis said we are experiencing a transition from a textual era, so we are thinking differently, but that doesn't mean that the physiology of our brains is different:

> *Before the press, information was passed mouth-to-ear, scribe-to-scribe; it was changed in the process; there was little sense of ownership and authorship. In the five-century-long Gutenberg era, text did set how we see our world: serially with a neat beginning and a defined end; permanent; authored. Now, we are passing out of this textual era and that may well affect how we look at our world. That may appear to change how we think. But it won't change our wires.*[6]

## Addiction

In January 2013, two girls from California were so desperate to stay online after 10 p.m. that they drugged their parents' milkshakes.[7] In April 2013 the newspapers were full of headlines about four-year-olds so addicted to iPads, computer games, and other technology that they required therapy, and they threw "iPaddies" when the technology was taken away from them. The story, across the newspapers, focused on Dr Richard Graham, who charges up to £16,000 for a twenty-eight-day "digital detox" programme to "cure addiction" at the Capio Nightingale Hospital in London.[8] In 2009, Chinese "internet addicts" (defined as spending over six hours a day online, and with no interest in school) were sent to military boot camps, although parents were also brought in to discuss their parenting techniques.[9]

The EU Kids Online project discovered that nearly half of the children questioned were happy to describe themselves as addicted (if no specific definition was offered), as in many ways the term is seen as a "badge of honour". It was also found that only about 10 per cent demonstrated true signs of addiction.[10]

But if children appear to be playing online excessively (every day, for long periods, sacrificing other activities) and it's affecting their mood, it is worth investigating further:

• • • • • • • • • • • • • • • • • • • • • • • • • • • • • • • • • •

> [Games are] so addictive; once they have used a game — educational or otherwise — that is all they want to do. We have to set definite boundaries on when or how often the technology can be used or risk being repeatedly pestered. Sometimes it feels easier just not to introduce them to it at all.
>
> **(Parent, 2 or under, 3 to 5, 6 to 9)**

From 2006 the term "internet addiction" started to appear, with reference to repetitive, compulsive, and uncontrollable use of technology. It was defined as an official disorder in 2012, with symptoms similar to other addictions,[11] although the origins of the problem need to be investigated more widely than the technology itself. Some teens get frustrated by how attached their friends and parents are to their own devices, wishing they would pay more attention to the person they are hanging out with.[12] Antony Mayfield, a digital consultant, notes that we like to pretend that we're in thrall to our machines: "Oh, I must take this call", but the machines don't care what we do. As I outlined in "Meet @drbexl", when we first got a TV I was rather obsessed with anything on it.

> *Sometimes a mild obsession can be helpful while you become literate in a new medium, but then you need to be able to make it work in terms which fit in with whatever you want to do with your life.*[13]

### The core signs of addiction
- *The activity becomes the most important thing in a person's life.*
- *Moods change in accordance with the activity.*

- *Continually higher doses of an activity are required to achieve the original sensations.*
- *Withdrawal symptoms such as anxiety and depression are experienced when the activity is stopped.*
- *Increasing conflict occurs with those in the closest social circle.*
- *There is a tendency to return to the activity after periods of control (relapse).*
- *The "sunk cost" fallacy is experienced: not wanting to abandon something after so much time has been sunk into it.*

Don Tapscott, author of *Net Generation*, pointed out in 1998 that "people do not talk about book addiction but rather use more positive terms such as voracious readers to describe children who spend time on this hobby", whereas with computers the talk is always of "addiction".[14] When children spend time playing on their computer it can be a good break from the "time-disciplined" focus of school and exam pressures, while a computer in their own room can allow them to escape marital conflicts, nags, chores, and siblings.

Still think your child has a problem? Don't panic. Sit down and discuss your concerns with them, having spoken to other parents and teachers within their peer group if it helps to understand what is "normal" for your child. If necessary, seek software to limit time online, such as ENUFF,[15] and, failing that, start to think about involving psychiatrists, and the best way to obtain their help will probably be through your GP.[16] Ensure that this is undertaken on a child-by-child basis, and that other children are not penalized for the behaviour of the one with the problem.

### Affecting schoolwork?

Even if your children are not truly addicted, it's still wise to consider how much time they spend online. Does the family agree about this, and how late at night is acceptable? Do children have their devices in their rooms? Do they hear the text bleep all night, or see the flash of the battery charger? Several doctors from the US-based National Sleep Foundation (NSF) have explained that the presence of technology and exposure to artificial light before going to bed can increase alertness and suppress the release of melatonin, which is an essential sleep-promoting hormone. An NSF study highlighted that nearly 95 per cent of those they surveyed were using some type of electronic device in the hour before going to bed, with two-thirds admitting that they weren't getting enough sleep during the week.[17]

*Some of the boundaries enforced by questionnaire respondents include:*

. . . . . . . . . . . . . . . . . . . . . . . . . . . . . . . . . . .

The children are not allowed game/computer access after 7 p.m. and before school.
**(Parent, 10 to 12)**

. . . . . . . . . . . . . . . . . . . . . . . . . . . . . . . . . . .

Mobile phones are put on a bookshelf after school and given back for an hour in the evening after dinner, as long as homework is done. (Still working on this one: doesn't always work very well!)
**(Parent, 6 to 9, 13 to 15)**

. . . . . . . . . . . . . . . . . . . . . . . . . . . . . . . . . . .

Router is generally turned off at 10.30 p.m. (which causes people to gather); discussions round the tea table; installation of website-monitoring software.
**(Parent, 13 to 15, 16 to 18, 19 or over)**

Teachers have remarked that lack of sleep affects academic performance the following day. Think about what kind of policies will fit within your family agreement in order to enforce good bedtimes and time limits on technology, and enable differentiation between screen use for homework and relaxation. Neuroscientist Dr Howard-Jones says: "Most parents would discourage their children from having a midnight chat to friends on the doorstep, but having access to a mobile phone under the duvet can also be a bad idea."[18] Australian paediatric sleep specialist Dr Seton wants schools to be careful about the amount of homework they set, to ensure that not all children's time is screen-focused.[19]

## Attention spans and multitasking

By the age of eleven, the majority of children are online for two hours or more every day. For younger children, those visits tend to be driven by a specific activity, but many of the older ones have online sources on constantly, multitasking with them in the background. Younger children are more likely to be sharing their machine and to have a greater range of activities that require time. "Multitasking" is often described as something new to "millennials", but Gina Maranto from the University of Miami says that information multitasking is not a new phenomenon: "My father, a corporate editor, used to watch television, read magazines, and listen to the radio at the same time long before computers, cell phones, or iPads."[20]

Professor Livingstone defines two different types of multitasking:

- Constructive: having Instant Messenger, music or search open, which contributes to something they are working on
- Distractive: watching TV on demand, videos, or playing games, which pulls them away from study.[21]

## Conversational ability

In the 1990s, teenage internet use was linked with social isolation, and these fears have continued to affect thinking since then. We can understand the concerns about the effects on communication skills, but early websites were difficult to use, very different from the technology that exists now. Most children are using online tools for social activities, often with their local friends, the equivalent of us rushing home to phone our friends when we were younger, while playing on our gaming devices. Think:

*If someone is spending a large portion of their time being social with people who live thousands of miles away, you can't say they've turned inward. They aren't shunning society. They're actively seeking it. They're probably doing it more actively than anyone around them.*[22]

*Questionnaire respondents were asked what their fears were for their children online:*

• • • • • • • • • • • • • • • • • • • • • • • • • • • • • • • • •

Too much time spent on their own, engaged in virtual conversations and activities. Not enough time spent learning active skills. Forgotten skills of letter writing and conversation over the phone with a real person.
**(Parent, 19 or over)**

• • • • • • • • • • • • • • • • • • • • • • • • • • • • • • • • •

Too easy for them to switch off from those around them and spend time on social network sites instead of interacting with people around them. It causes behavioural problems when you try to encourage them to "unplug".
**(Parent, 16 to 18, 19 or over)**

• • • • • • • • • • • • • • • • • • • • • • • • • • • • • • • • •

They can disengage from those around them and become lost in their own private world, with their headphones in their ears. On the school bus

apparently most people have their headphones in and
this means that real interactions with others are
diminished.
**(Parent, 10 to 12)**

Ever since the invention of the Walkman in the 1970s there have been concerns that children will disconnect. There were worries that the school bus journey was a space in which communication skills were learned, including how to deal with conflict. Many children now, however, travel by other means and spend ages in the playground, so what has really changed for them when it comes to socializing?

Children, as always, will use a broad range of approaches to communication, choosing different methods according to purpose. Although in some cases social media can be seen as a trade-off with time they could be spending with friends face to face, most simply see it as part of their communication mix, and would choose face-to-face conversation for something serious. Quick chats and social arrangements involve more use of texts, which are quick and easy, and if it is something more complicated, they give them more time to think about how to respond, which they can do without being overheard.[23]

• • • • • • • • • • • • • • • • • • • • • • • • • • • • • • • • • • •

The biggest positive [of digital media] is the
development of an intuitive understanding of the way
the world will continue to engage and communicate,
as well as allowing an outgoing, extroverted only
child to maintain engagement with friends while
physically on their own.
**(Parent, 10 to 12)**

In *The Guardian*, Amanda Lenhart from Pew Internet puts it another way:

*Our research shows face-to-face time between teenagers hasn't changed over the past five years. Technology has simply added another layer on top. Yes, you can find studies that suggest online networking can be bad for you. But there are just as many that show the opposite.*[24]

Teachers and school governors are concerned that an increasing number of children are starting school without the expected level of conversational ability. The consensus is that this is not because *they* are spending time on technology, but because their parents are. I have heard of a few cases where teaching assistants have been asked to run remedial conversation classes for infants who have come to school unable to talk properly, because their parents have been plugged into technology all the children's lives. Researchers observing behaviour in Disney's theme parks noted that what most captured the young children's attention wasn't Disney-conjured magic but their parents' mobile phones, as they saw that that was where their attention was, and they wanted some of it.[25]

On Parents.com, the statistics demonstrate that "at age 2, most children know 20 to 200 words; by age 3, that number soars to about 1,000". This is achieved, however, only with input from parents. They need to encourage their children to chat, says Janet Felice, a speech–language pathologist: "When kids start school, teachers expect them to have a pretty strong vocabulary. If your child doesn't develop a solid foundation as a toddler, he may struggle to keep up with the class."[26]

### Couch potatoes?

The CHILDWISE "Digital Lives" Report (2010), which interviewed only keen internet users, noted that all these children had a wide range of other interests, including time with friends, family, shopping, and the outdoors. The 2013 CHILDWISE Report demonstrated that 84 per cent still played sport outside compulsory school sessions, with an average of three hours a week on top of two and a half at school.[27] We need to understand, too, that it's not either a computer or the outdoors any more: with mobile devices it can be both. Outdoor activities that involve digital devices include geocaching https://www.geocaching.com (a digital treasure hunt using GPS), or learning about "wild things" in your local area, e.g. http://www.projectwildthing.com/#app, which uses geolocation to encourage kids back into nature, or piques their imagination by reading about elephants before visiting/at the zoo. Before blaming the technology, think about what other factors might be involved:

• • • • • • • • • • • • • • • • • • • • • • • • • • • • • • • • • • •

They spend a lot more time on their own interacting with other people virtually rather than in real life. My youngest child spends a lot less time getting exercise or in the fresh air, though that may partly be an aspect of his personality rather than solely the fault of technology.

**(Parent, 16 to 18, 19 or over)**

In 2013 Professor Lydia Plowman from the University of Edinburgh challenged the idea that we are breeding a generation of couch potatoes:

*Many people feel that the domination of children's lives by technology means they don't get enough exercise, or spend enough time playing. However, our research showed that technology doesn't influence day-to-day life for children of this age as much as its ubiquity might suggest.*

Professor Plowman was being quoted in an article in *The Scotsman*, which emphasized that it's all about balance, and that some children might need some "encouragement" to go outside.[28]

# 13

# Screen Time and Family Dynamics

When computers were first introduced in the 1970s, they were complicated and limited to the workplace of the technologically inclined. In the 1980s/90s, as the government sought to put computers in every classroom, PC companies decided to advertise to the domestic market and to make the idea of providing a computer in the home seem normal, as part of giving children the best start in life. The same message is now being applied to the latest technologies such as smartphones or tablet devices.

*Questionnaire respondents were asked if they had any particular limitations in place. Several mentioned screen-time limits:*

• • • • • • • • • • • • • • • • • • • • • • • • • • • • • • • • • • • •

Supervised use, discussions about what's appropriate to put on blogs, etc. We limit iPad and game time to after lunch and only for thirty minutes at a time (for example).

**(Parent, 3 to 5, 6 to 9)**

• • • • • • • • • • • • • • • • • • • • • • • • • • • • • • • •

We put time restrictions on the use of all screens. This seems to work in the family. All homework is done before any screen time.

**(Parent, 6 to 9)**


• • • • • • • • • • • • • • • • • • • • • • • • • • • • • • • •

We had agreements about how much time my daughter could go online, hotly contested almost every evening. There is a huge temptation to simply give in and say "Just do what you want", because it would be easier.

**(Parent, 19+)**


• • • • • • • • • • • • • • • • • • • • • • • • • • • • • • • •

Discussions, good relationships, and supervised use seem to be working so far (i.e. he only uses screens in family rooms and asks before he goes on certain sites).

**(Parent, 10 to 12)**


Research in 1994 logged the way children spent their time. It was noted that the location of computer use was changing from the local library to at home, so children were spending more time at home. Family dynamics did not change as feared because of computer use at home, as children tended to be replacing TV-watching time with computers, rather than other activities.[1] OXIS research highlighted that the internet most often complements other forms of contact.[2]

### Recommended screen time

Ever since the 1999 American Academy of Pediatrics discouraged television viewing for children younger than two, citing that age group's critical need for "direct interaction with parents" and others, we've been left with the impression that screen time is bad.[3] As Hanna Rosin, a technology journalist, notes, such statements assume that an hour spent watching TV is an hour not spent doing something deemed more constructive, but, as we've already seen, most children continue to have a varied range of activities. She was visiting a developers' conference, anticipating that she would get some up-to-date guidance on screen use. She found, however, that most were proffering the same old advice, with rules including no screen time during the week, no more than half an hour a day, only on long journeys, and never use it as an e-babysitter – although one excused this as educational: "I only let her watch movies in Spanish."[4]

· · · · · · · · · · · · · · · · · · · · · · · · · · · · · · · · · · · · ·

We agree on no more than thirty minutes a day of any technology, and we never let our children use the internet unsupervised.

**(Parent, 2 or under, 3 to 5, 6 to 9)**

· · · · · · · · · · · · · · · · · · · · · · · · · · · · · · · · · · · · ·

Parents feel very pressured to allow their children a lot of access. We take the view that much of this access is a privilege and not a right, and that frames our family usage.

**(Parent, 6 to 9, 13 to 15)**

The CHILDWISE Monitor Report 2012 indicates that most children over five are getting somewhere between four and eight hours of total screen time per day, including TV, the internet, games consoles, and mobile phones. The average time spent on the internet has remained constant at around two and a half hours over the last four to five years, although an increasing number are looking at two or three screens at once. The largest amounts of time spent online involve social networking and gaming.

In March 2013, the Medical Research Council in Glasgow published the results of a study involving over 11,000 children, which explored possible links between behavioural problems and children's screen time. "It found little direct connection between the two once other factors such as parental attitudes and wellbeing had been taken into consideration."[5]

Some parents are happy that their children spend so much time online because it shows they are passionate about something. Parents should be encouraged to help their children identify websites that encourage their passions. For example, it has been seen that those who watch online football will probably want to go out and try the game for themselves. Other parents recommend that families plan their screen time, suggesting a monthly day of no screens, screen-free time from 10 a.m. to 6 p.m. in school holidays, and/or no screens in bedrooms after 9 p.m. One CHILDWISE 2012 statistic that parents may be interested in is that "those who access the Internet in their own room spend an average of two hours a day online, those accessing elsewhere at home use for just one hour a day on average".

## Bedroom culture

These days many families have at least one computer at home, but an increasing number have multiple computers, including some in children's bedrooms. With the development of Wi-Fi and laptops, young children are often sitting next to their parents on the sofa while others are in the privacy of their own room.[6]

*Many questionnaire respondents offered comments regarding the location of internet use within the home:*

• • • • • • • • • • • • • • • • • • • • • • • • • • • • • • • • • •

So far, we are happy with the measures we have taken. The home PC is downstairs in the office and so children and screen are in plain sight when online. We have safe settings on Google – although appreciate that this could easily be changed by an older child if they wanted to! We encourage openness and discussion of things that come up while searching or in chat rooms, and have talked about internet safety together with the children. We don't supervise use directly, but have a good idea of what our children are doing online.

**(Parent, 6 to 9, 10 to 12)**

· · · · · · · · · · · · · · · · · · · · · · · · · · · · · · · · · · · ·

We anticipate that as our children get older we will be under more pressure for them to engage in social media and especially to have digital technology in their bedrooms. We plan to discourage this, with a family agreement to keep digital technology downstairs so that our bedrooms are reserved for sleeping.

**(Parent, 6 to 9, 10 to 12)**

· · · · · · · · · · · · · · · · · · · · · · · · · · · · · · · · · · · ·

We recommend the following guidelines: until they are eighteen, limit use of laptops in bedrooms. Keep doors open and screens visible to the rest of the family. Encourage discussion with kids about stalkers, inappropriate web use, best practice, etc.

**(Parent, 13 to 15, 16 to 18, 19 or over)**

Industrialization led to the separation of home and work, with home becoming a "sacred" space for the family. We nostalgically "remember" that with increased leisure time the family could get together in communal spaces and over meals, and visibly see themselves as a family... and then the TV came along! For many, however, that was the glue that kept the family together, discussing the TV programmes they watched. Now, with the computer, parents and children can look up information together, or, as we now have such portable devices, the child could just be working on the computer in the kitchen while dinner is being cooked. In recent years, however, the "outside world" has come to be seen as increasingly risky, and children's (independent) access to it has become correspondingly restricted. When people complain about "bedroom culture", they need to realize that it is part of these wider changes in society. There are then further fears that children will think that they don't need to leave their room because they have everything they want on their electronic devices, though if they are thinking like that there are probably questions that need to be asked about their offline relationships.

## Digital time out

*Questionnaire respondents were asked what they feared from digital technology, and practices they had in place for managing it:*

- - - - - - - - - - - - - - - - - - - - - - - - - - - - - - - - - - - -

A tendency to be engaged with a community other than the physical one they are in, i.e. the family around them.

**(Parent, 13 to 15, 16 to 18)**

- - - - - - - - - - - - - - - - - - - - - - - - - - - - - - - - - - - -

We are able to spend frequent holidays away from home and rarely take the internet with us (no connection at our holiday home!), which helps us keep things in perspective (at least, it did until we had smartphones!).

**(Parent, 16 to 18)**

As technology has affected our leisure time, so it also makes it more difficult for teenagers and adults to break off from other aspects of life, including work. Professor Sherry Turkle, author of *Alone Together*, believes that digital media affect our ability to give full, undistracted attention to each other or to our thoughts. She claims that lack of disconnected downtime disrupts ties to other people and adds emotional stress. In conversation with eighteen-year-olds, she asked when they last were able to be free of interruptions, but they didn't see digital media as interruptions but as the beginning of connections. Research indicates that a large number of teenagers would love to be able to unplug, especially as they feel that their online communications are being so heavily monitored. A significant number, however, said that this would make them feel more stressed, because they have invested so much time in their "digital space", and even more because their parents fear letting them out of the door.

Some have tested extreme detoxes. Susan Maushart, writing for the *Daily Mail*, undertook a six-month "technology blackout" for her entire family, which she viewed as a consciousness-raising exercise rather than a long-term strategy.[7] Paul Millar, a technology journalist, disconnected from the internet for a year but found that, after the initial feeling of "freedom", he picked up other bad habits. He ignored his post and his friends, allowed the dust to gather on his exercise equipment, failed to turn boredom into creativity, and sat and did nothing. On analysing this for an article for *The Verge* magazine, he was able to make more informed technology choices once he reconnected.[8]

### Reading online

With the growth of tablet devices and e-readers, one of the leading debates is about both the quality and the quantity of reading. The CHILDWISE 2012 Report points to the 30 per cent that read often for pleasure, although 17 per cent never do so, with 14 per cent of boys and 11 per cent of girls favouring e-books over printed books:

*At age 7–8, children are becoming confident, established readers, but do not have the entrenched familiarity with traditional books that exists among older children.*

With technological developments such as flowable text and full colour, e-readers have become a more appealing prospect, especially for children of eleven plus. Sarah Odedina, Managing Director of Hot Key Books, a publisher of children's fiction, says:

*It is entirely possible that people will be more used to reading from a screen than a page, and I do not think it matters in the least, so long as they are reading.*[9]

Baroness Greenfield, a neuroscientist, agreed with the National Literacy Trust (NLT) that there is "no conclusive evidence that reading standards are deteriorating", as reading from a screen is just as good as reading from a book. NLT director Jonathan Douglas added that the growth in children's digital reading was "an opportunity for publishers, not a warning knell", and said the children's market was beginning to mirror the way the adult market has developed as the number of children reading digitally increases. He also said there was a "clear relationship between attainment and reading patterns", with those children with a "balanced diet of print and digital" achieving a higher level of literacy.[10]

Hanna Rosin challenges the notion that books are inherently better than screens, observing that her daughter tends to use books to avoid social interaction, whilst her son uses the Wii to connect with friends.

Some parents have responded by treating digital technology the same way as other toys, lumping them all together in one basket. The child can play with whatever they choose from the basket. For a couple of weeks they spend hours on the digital device, as they would with any other toy, then it falls out of rotation as every other toy does, and is forgotten for several weeks.[11]

Effective practice includes encouraging children to see their media use as a healthy part of their whole range of activities. One of my friends has a pot full of lolly sticks, each one with a different activity on it, some of which are screen-related. What makes me laugh is when she posts on Facebook that one of them has pulled out the one that says "Tidy the Lounge"![12]

# Gaming

I've never been a gamer, aside from a few games of *Pac-Man*, *Tetris*, *Angry Birds*, and *Candy Crush*. In 2011, £1.35 billion was spent in the UK on console video-game software, particularly for boys, although an increasing number of girls are playing on apps. On Christmas Day 2011, *Angry Birds* was downloaded 6.5 million times,[1] and thousands play Facebook games such as *Cityville* and *Candy Crush*. Gaming is one of the digital areas that has been least researched so far, although the term "gamification" has really taken off in education, where game principles are applied to learning. It is recognized that children learn more in this way because they are enjoying themselves, and because they are engaged in what they are doing.[2]

• • • • • • • • • • • • • • • • • • • • • • • • • • • • • • • • •

Homework is done online, e.g. *My Maths*. They get instant feedback on whether they've got it right. *Professor Layton* was a great game to start them reading, and solving puzzles, with a longer attention span required. YouTube videos of those experiments Mum won't let you do in the kitchen and *The Slow Mo Guys* make science really fun, especially when school science is all filling in answer sheets and nothing hands-on.

**(Parent, 10 to 12, 13 to 15)**

You'll probably recognize the names of some of the most popular games for children: *Moshi Monsters, Club Penguin, Bin Weevils, MyCBBC, Farmville, HABBO Hotel, Stardoll, BuildaBearville, World of Warcraft, Runescape* and *Neopets*. Games such as *Medal of Honor* have raised concerns because massive multiplayer games like this are so immersive that players may start to identify strongly with the political objectives of the group that they are role-playing, such as the Taliban. EA, the producers of the game, withdrew it in January 2013 because it wasn't selling too well, unlike their bestseller *FIFA13*.[3] Note that the game was pulled because of poor sales (despite the publicity), so let your wallet speak to the manufacturers. If your child does have some of these games, however, discuss limits, as these parents have done:

· · · · · · · · · · · · · · · · · · · · · · · · · · · · · · · · · · ·

Recently we put limits on the playing of *Minecraft*, and one parent let us know she was glad we had set some boundaries. I hadn't thought through the impact of our family boundaries on other families; I just knew we didn't want our child playing on it to the extent he was.

**(Parent, 6 to 9, 10 to 12, 13 to 15)**

*Some questionnaire respondents put forward suggestions of benefits that their children had obtained from gaming:*

· · · · · · · · · · · · · · · · · · · · · · · · · · · · · · · · · · ·

Our children have developed an ability to socialize easily out of school with lots of different friends. Their shared interest in *Minecraft* has enabled our younger son to make contact with a boy from Australia (through online gaming).

**(Parent, 10 to 12, 13 to 15)**

> Our teenage son interacts with his friends via a
> game, *Minecraft*; this has benefits, but I do have
> concerns that it can become very time-consuming.
> **(Parent, 6 to 9, 10 to 12, 13 to 15)**

If you want to understand the different types of game, I've attempted to summarize the guidance from the Institute of Education for site moderators:[4]

- ***Three-dimensional (3D) virtual worlds*** such as *Second Life* provide virtual spaces in which users interact using 3D avatars. They can be based on real-world or imaginary environments.

- ***Web-based online games*** are usually relatively casual games designed for shorter play sessions, and have limited interactivity with other players but offer rewards for continued participation. Games such as *Candy Crush* on Facebook would fall into this category.

- ***Online PC games*** are downloaded or distributed via CD or DVD; they are more elaborate than web-based games (so heavy on the graphics card), with more in-game interaction with other players.

- ***Console-based online games*** are played on TV-based consoles and hand-held or mobile devices, each of which offers an online service connecting users of its console, such as Xbox Live. Players can connect with others of similar ability or language to play together, and are increasingly linked with social networks.

- ***Multiplayer games***, which can be on any platform, typically connect a few players for the length of a single play session. For example a sports game played online might pit a player against other human players rather than artificial opponents controlled by the PC or games console.

- ***Massively multiplayer online games (MMOG)***, such as *World of Warcraft*, create an ongoing world. Players create a character and will expect to play this for several months, with many other players.

**EXERCISE: Look at a range of potential games, and discuss what might be gained from them and what needs more care.**

## Finding age-appropriate games

In 1998 PEGI was formed as a ratings system for games, although most parents seem to use rules/ratings systems for guidance rather than as absolutes, with the ratings enabling them to make an informed choice.[5]

· · · · · · · · · · · · · · · · · · · · · · · · · · · · · · · · · · · · · · · ·

We are strict in some respects (film/game age ratings) but do trust our children within reason when online. They always come to check whether they are allowed on a certain website, and (although moaning that it's not fair) they respect our decision.

**(Parent, 10 to 12)**

The Byron Review (2008) was keen to ensure that parents felt informed and confident about assessing the levels of risk in games for their children. The voices of these better-informed parents can then drive industry investment and continued innovation in the area of child safety in video games.

· · · · · · · · · · · · · · · · · · · · · · · · · · · · · · · · · · · · · · · ·

They see a lot more violence and sexual imagery than we had access to years ago, and many of the games they play include killing and swearing, even though we have always tried to maintain age-appropriate contact. We can no longer police our children's use of their e-devices; their expertise and familiarity far exceed our own capabilities.

**(Parent, 16 to 18, 19 or over)**

Games are clearly aimed at one gender or the other, with girls' games tending to be pink or purple, focusing on dressing up, celebrities, and animals, whereas boys' games tend to be blue and focus on sport, action, and driving. It is easy for children to discover the games that they want, often hearing about them at friends'/cousins' houses, or through a simple search on Google.

*Help with choosing appropriate games:*
- *http://www.pegi.info/, including this brief guide: http://www. pegi.info/en/index/id/media/pdf/241.pdf*
- *http://www.commonsensemedia.org/game-reviews*

## The positives of gaming

Shawn Marie Edgington, creator of the One-Click-Safety series, claims that more sociable children are found on sites such as Facebook, while those who are less sociable migrate towards games.[6] The evidence from the CHILDWISE 2012 Report, however, is that playing games with others, and chatting to friends via in-game means, are the most popular activities on games consoles, because children can try out things they couldn't do "for real". Journalist Pamela Whitby discovered that children who play games for an average of two hours per day have a wider circle of friends, do more physical activity, and do more homework than others, although those who spend more time than that demonstrate less fitness and more social isolation.[7]

*Byron, Children's Call for Evidence, 2008*
*One of the reasons I enjoy playing video games online is that I can interact with people from all over the world and make friends. Most online games have groups of players working together to complete objectives, which can improve team and leadership skills, or just for socialising while playing the game. Some of my best friends are online ones.*

*I play video games for the same reason I watch a film or TV, escapism, the chance to be immersed in an intriguing or exciting story.[8]*

As with all the activities that your child engages in, undertake some research into the games they wish to play, and don't assume they are inherently bad. Gaming can develop particular skills, including the solving of complex problems, collaboration, quick reactions, and learning how to customize games, such as by designing new levels:

> [C]reators had inserted hacks, shortcuts, and trapdoors for players to ferret out – or learn of from friends. "The evolution of games started to mimic the complexity of real life," Wong says. "Life doesn't come to you in a box with an instruction book."[9]

Derek Brown, Digital Editor for the *Sun*, plays games with his daughter, often *Lego City*. The game takes time:

> At times, she says she's bored with the game and wants to play something else, but I, in a sort of Victorian dad way, insist we see this thing through. Why? Well, I think the importance of learning to finish something you've started has been lost in a world where there are so many quick distractions like YouTube, Twitter, texting and BBM.

A study at Brigham Young University, Utah, found that girls who regularly play video games with their dads are happier and healthier and have a much better relationship with their parents, and are far less likely to get depressed in their adolescent years.[10] But this may just be because they are spending time with their fathers, rather than because of the particular technology involved.

· · · · · · · · · · · · · · · · · · · · · · · · · · · · · · · · · ·

It's important to be present with your kids, wherever they are. I have listened to many extended disquisitions on Magic the Gathering, dub stepping, knot tying, and all kinds of other YouTube-inspired stuff that I couldn't care less about. But I care about HIM.

**(Parent, 10 to 12)**

## Violent, addictive, and expensive?

It's clear that game developers have taken the time to learn about human psychology: what will cause us to "play just one more level" and in the process lose several hours (or even days/weeks) of our lives, as well as large sums of money (many games are initially free, but you pay for in-game purchases, which can quickly add up). Again, technology magazine *The Next Web* raises the question of whether "addiction" is the right term:

> *Why do we stigmatize certain engrossments more than others? When my kid reads books all day, my partner and I are happy about it. When he plays games all day, we are not. Who is to say one is better or worse than the other?*[11]

Author Michael Carr-Gregg, however, shows how game manufacturers entice users in with a mix of sex and violence. The more outrage a game provokes in the papers, including MMORPGs (Massively Multiplayer Online Role-Playing Games) such as *World of Warcraft,* the more it sells. These games have no ultimate goal, so there's no specific end to them, with add-ons and opportunities for in-world chat. The games are designed to reward those who put in the hours online. There is a real danger of the "compulsive loop".[12] Some Asian game players have died because they ignored their bodily signals in pursuit of the game, which may be why one Chinese father hired "in-game assassins". Professor Mark Griffiths, a gambling and addictions expert at Nottingham Trent University, commented:

*It's not going to do much for family relations, I've never
heard of that kind of intervention before, but I don't think
these top-down approaches work. Most excessive game
playing is usually a symptom of an underlying problem.*[13]

Dr Micah Mazurek from the University of Missouri undertook
research into video games for children on the autism spectrum.
She found that children with ASD (Autism Spectrum Disorders)
spent more time playing video games than typically developing
children did, and were much more likely to develop problematic
or addictive patterns of video-game play. But, there is also
evidence among such children of an increased development of
social skills, although research is required to see whether these
translate outside the game environment.[14]

As always, the best advice is to know your own child, know
what they are safe to be left to play, and determine time limits,
such as a maximum of one hour for each weekday, two hours at
weekends, and nothing at all until homework or housework is
finished. If you are an avid gamer, think about what your own
behaviour says, and take the time to test out games before your
children use them. Curiosity, vicarious thrills, fascination, and
the pure entertainment value of fight games are all valid and
normal, and children will have already seen these things on
TV. Working with your children gives you an opportunity to
encourage them to think critically about their own behaviour,
how it affects others, and what they choose to watch.[15]

**Privacy settings for consoles:**

- *Xbox Live: http://www.youtube.com/watch?v=NU8hr43cu4Y*
- *Nintendo: http://www.nintendo.com/consumer/info/en_na/
parents.jsp*
- *Playstation: http://uk.playstation.com/psn/support/ps3/detail/
linked235311/item435783/PlayStation-Network-Privacy-settings/*

# 15

# Does Digital Offer Life Opportunities?

In October 2012, a survey of 2,000 people for *Tonight* (ITV) claimed that 62 per cent of those questioned believed technology had changed their life for the better.[1] In 1995, Tony Blair said:

*Technology has revolutionised the way we work and is now set to transform education. Children cannot be effective in tomorrow's world if they are trained in yesterday's skills.*[2]

Children need to acquire "social capital", as this gives them access to opportunities in education and the labour market. Social networks (and not just the digital ones) are part of this system of social capital in which young people have to be recognized as valid and valued contributors. Elizabeth Ribbans, a news editor for *The Guardian,* recently gave a talk to schoolchildren from a disadvantaged area and afterwards said that,

*The one strong thing that came out of it from them was they thought they were either in the news for something*

*bad (crime, drugs, etc.) or something good (sports or exam results), but that for the vast majority of them, they are never written about.[3]*

Questionnaire respondents highlighted why it was important for their children to be engaged online:

• • • • • • • • • • • • • • • • • • • • • • • • • • • • • • • • •

Today's workplace requires the ability to use this technology and so it is good that they grow up with it.

**(Parent, 6 to 9)**

• • • • • • • • • • • • • • • • • • • • • • • • • • • • • • • •

It gives them direct access to leaders in the field, access to a wealth of information, and the ability to communicate instantly with people around the world of different cultures and experiences. My kids are motivated by technology; they write blogs, read books, and complete complex maths, often with games, or the promise of games, once questions are answered.

**(Parent/School IT manager, 6 to 9, 10 to 12)**

It's worth taking time to discuss what standards your children would like to see established to ensure that things are beneficial for all members of the community. Encourage them to think about digital citizenship,[4] and to participate in the EU-wide Safer Internet Day (February, annually).[5] It's OK to "lurk" online as you learn the processes: watch and observe others. Over time, newbies learn and develop expertise and become more central to the community and its activities, but are also shaped by their participation in communities.[6]

## Criticality and avoiding the scams

With so much user-generated content online, and because fraudsters have decided the online space is worth focusing energy on, we need to help children become able to exercise critical judgment about the information they read online, and avoid being drawn into scams. Digital literacy, referred to at the beginning of this book, means more than distinguishing between reliable and unreliable sources. It also includes considering the questions of who, what, where, why, and how the content has been produced, and for what purpose. The Canadian MediaSmarts research (2012) highlighted that most survey respondents (teenagers) assumed that online companies were seeking to "trick" them into releasing information. However, the respondents showed a strong critical understanding of many of the popular cultural images they encountered. They often made decisions about the kind of content they did not want to see because it made them uncomfortable.

"Phishing" emails direct you to a website that looks like the real website of a store or financial institution, and are designed solely to encourage you to reveal personal or financial details, "phishing" for information such as your credit card numbers, account names, passwords, and other personal information.[7] Willard looked back to a study into phishing, in which twenty-seven links were shared, of which only seven were legitimate. She found that adults were easily fooled, largely because they went by how the site *looked* rather than by how they had got to the site, which is the most effective way of establishing legitimacy. Following a link in an email is rarely a safe bet: use a search engine instead, and report the fake to the genuine site. It's also worth taking simple steps to avoid identity theft, and the National Crime Prevention Council (US) provides such advice.[8]

Something else to look out for: free giveaways (especially Apple products) and some "tug-at-the-heartstring" stories on Facebook:[9]

*From our research, we have found that the most likely reason such fake promotions are created is to simply build up a Facebook page with massive amounts of likes. These pages are then sold, renamed, and all traces of their fake promotions are deleted.*[10]

I tend not to share these pages (especially after checking on the sites below) but rather to put a comment on the page of the Facebook friend who has shared it, to the effect that it's fake, to prevent others from being caught out.

### Check the legitimacy:
- *Snopes: http://www.snopes.com*
- *Facecrooks: http://facecrooks.com*
- *Phishing: http://www.microsoft.com/en-gb/security/online-privacy/phishing-symptoms.aspx*
- *ID theft: http://www.actionfraud.police.uk/fraud_protection/identity_fraud*

One thing that I've noticed in my university students is that many of them will first go to Google (especially Google Scholar) and Amazon to do research for essays, although they are encouraged also to talk to the library about online access to journals. Libraries are increasingly lining up e-books that can be "hired" by students, while still retaining print books. Students, however, have had little training in using digital tools for educational purposes (rather than just as social tools), and require lessons in how to be more critical about the information that they are finding online. Research papers given at conferences have also highlighted that although students can "talk the talk" as far as the digital is concerned, when their online actions are observed, their search skills are very poor. They tend to seize upon the first bit of information they find, assuming that they have discovered the "right" answer, rather than critiquing the source. I'm sure people used to do the same with books! It is important to point out that a "critique" shouldn't just focus on the negative: it's about pointing out strengths as much as weaknesses.[11]

Students also need to be aware of the particular nature of search engines and online encyclopaedias. Search engines, including Google, are commercial concerns, and this may affect the rankings and returns that they get, so using search engines to cross-reference and seek additional information is helpful. Many students will also head straight for Wikipedia. It has much to recommend it as a starting point, especially now that all sources have to be cited, so can be followed up. Its entries are only as credible as their sources, however, and Wikipedia constantly works to increase credibility, while maintaining an open user-contributed environment.[12] Care must also be taken with regard to the credibility of the writers of blogs, because if there is an error on an influential site, and that is copied and pasted elsewhere, it is perpetuated.[13] We need to learn to search with our eyes open.

**EXERCISE: Go to Wikipedia and search for something that you know a fair bit about. What information do you support, and what would you challenge?**

## Working together: collaboration

There's a lot of pressure on parents to raise children as strong, independent, and contributing citizens with strong social values. We need to think about what community and citizenship look like in a global world: who is our neighbour in this digital age, and how far do we need to take responsibility for the well-being of others?

Children who are reported for their bad digital behaviour (by friends or neighbours) learn a valuable lesson: nothing is private on the internet, not from your friends, your parents, or even from the parents of your friends. Look out for the children of your friends and neighbours, not by actively looking for wrongdoing, but by considering what you would do in the equivalent physical situation. If you would report it to their parents offline, then you probably should online.[14]

Collective intelligence, crowd-sourcing, smart mobs, and the "global brain" are some of the descriptive phrases tied to humans working together to accomplish things in a collaborative manner online. Internet researcher and software designer Fred Stutzman says this bodes well for those who are developing the skills:

*The sharing, tweeting, and status updating of today are preparing us for a future of ad hoc, always-on collaboration. The skills being honed on social networks today will be critical tomorrow, as work will be dominated by fast-moving, geographically diverse, free-agent teams of workers connected via socially mediating technologies.*[15]

• • • • • • • • • • • • • • • • • • • • • • • • • • • • • • • • • • • •

Digital content and access is vital: it is up to us as parents to ensure that ground rules are put in place and to monitor as much as we can.
**(Parent, 6 to 9, 16 to 18)**

### Clicktivism, activism, and social justice

The Byron Review (2008) highlighted how the internet can be a place for building community, particularly for building or renewing civic participation, generating tolerance and global understanding, and providing young people with a space to have a "voice". Some certainly show the traits that Don Tapscott believes "digital natives" have: using social networks to effect serious political change; an increasing awareness of social justice issues, caring more for integrity, and being tolerant of diversity. They are quick to condemn, but quick to forgive if they see that the offender is truly sorry for an error, and ask about values before they buy.[16]

I, however, would not say that all young people "naturally" exhibit these values, but there are certainly opportunities for those who are interested. There's the simple action of signing petitions on sites such as 38 degrees (but be sure to customize your entry and indicate why it's important, as more notice is then taken of your submission),[17] or joining large campaigns such as EnoughFoodIF.[18] At events such as the bombing of the Boston Marathon, social media users used the technology to offer practical help,[19] while the story that spread across Facebook in 2013 about "suspended coffees" (where customers can leave money for a coffee, and the shop then gives this to the next homeless person who comes in) led to a range of coffee shops taking up this practice.[20]

In February 2013, I went to Uganda with Tearfund on their first bloggers' trip, designed to raise awareness of the work that was being done, taking an "ordinary person's" perspective rather than that of a marketing person employed by the organization.[21] Inspired by this, I continue to look for ways to support the charity. It is important to think about the extent to which we are merely undertaking "Clicktivism", and what we need to do to turn it into "Activism". At a conference in 2010, social media consultant James Poulter asked what methods William Wilberforce would have used had he been seeking to end slavery today. Would he have used sites such as http://slaveryfootprint.org (where you can calculate how many are suffering for the goods that you buy)? Maybe, but he would almost certainly then have looked at the information that he had gained and decided what further action to take, and not stopped at an e-petition.

**EXERCISE: Talk to your child about a subject they are passionate about. Consider how the internet can help them to become more informed, and how they might begin to take action.**

# 16

# Some Thoughts for Others Working with Children

## Grandparents

The OXIS Survey of 2011 claimed: "The elderly, the retired and the poorly educated tend to be the least likely to use the internet, and they are the most fearful of technology 'breaking' or 'failing' when they need it most." I've always said that the keenest users of technology are those who have a purpose for doing so. Grandparents are joining social media in droves, using technology to support hobbies, build friendships, and stay in touch with their families.[1] A Vodafone survey in 2011 discovered that one in ten UK grandparents used technology every day to make contact with grandchildren, and 29 per cent would feel isolated from their family if they didn't have access to the internet.[2] According to Grandparentsplus.org.uk, four in five teenagers say grandparents are the most important people outside their immediate family.

- - - - - - - - - - - - - - - - - - - - - - - - - - - - - - - - - - - -

Their grandparents live far away and we only see
them once a year, so Skype calls are a great way for
them to keep in touch.
**(Parent, 3 to 5, 6 to 9)**

- - - - - - - - - - - - - - - - - - - - - - - - - - - - - - - - - - - -

They love to keep in touch with me by messaging [and
I can help] with spelling (well, I can understand
what they mean if they type too quickly and some of
the words are not quite correct!!).
**(Grandparent, 6 to 9)**

This new group of grandparents have particularly got to grips with texting, emailing, webcams, and sharing/viewing photos on social networks. Once they have tasted the online experience, many are tempted to develop their online skills further.

Many grandparents also look after their grandchildren and, whether it's for a short or a long time, need some understanding of the digital environment in order to best support them. Those who have been involved with children with special needs are particularly enthusiastic about the benefits of digital technology. "Not a grumpy old man" responded to the questionnaire with: "I have no influence over my grandchildren's use of technology but I trust their parents to get the balance correct."

- - - - - - - - - - - - - - - - - - - - - - - - - - - - - - - - - - - -

Use in the family, both at home and in their
grandparents' house, is supervised. Help is given in
making the best use of technology.
**(Parent, 6 to 9)**

Another Vodafone survey in October 2012 revealed that "8 per cent of parents said they are aware that their children are taking advantage of their grandparents' unfamiliarity with technology to, for example, access inappropriate content online, sign up to social networks or spend too much time on smartphones or tablets". They were seeking to encourage more of the type of response that I got, such as: "I chat with my daughter about any worries, but she has the final say as to what her children can and can't do" (Grandparent, 6 to 9). Others said that there was a family agreement with the parents, which the grandparents stuck to, supervising and supporting the use of the technology and not being afraid to remove devices from the grandchild.

Others are proactively embracing the new opportunities that digital technology brings. David Gee asked *The Guardian* for advice on purchasing a digital voice recorder to collect his parents' oral history so that the grandchildren could listen to it twenty years later, and was given a range of options and recommended to visit the New Zealand History site for a suggested list of questions to ask (http://www.nzhistory.net.nz/ pdfs/Life-history-questions.pdf).[3]

## Some further resources

- http://www.grandparentsplus.org.uk
  A national UK charity, keen to encourage the involvement of grandchildren in children's lives. It works particularly with those who take on an active caring role. A useful range of suggestions for (non-technological) activities to get children involved in: http://www.grandparentsplus. org.uk/things-children-five
- http://digitalunite.com/guides
  Formerly "Silver Surfers Online", this site provides a great series of guides to download, print off, and share, whether you're a first-time computer user or want to learn about social networking. There are also opportunities to undertake online courses or connect with an online tutor.
- http://www.gransnet.com/life-and-style/technology
  A UK-based online community launched in 2011,

offering plenty of opportunities to chat to other grandparents, but also providing help with topics such as online safety, getting on Facebook/Twitter, and apps grandparents might enjoy.

## Teachers

Schools and teachers are frequently identified as significant not only in ensuring children's safety online, but also in helping students to become digitally literate.

· · · · · · · · · · · · · · · · · · · · · · · · · · · · · · · · · · · ·

We have no control over the discussions our children are having at school about technologies. We need our schools and educators to take a strong lead in telling children what is good practice and things to be aware of. As parents we don't always know what they should be aware of. Technology is SO market driven that we can't keep up.

**(Parent, 19 or over)**

As secondary school teacher Louise Upchurch points out, students spend far more time outside school than inside it, and therefore all parties (parents, students, and teachers) need to be involved in discussions about school digital policies to ensure a joined-up approach at both home and school. In return, parents need to keep teachers in the loop about external issues that may affect their children in school, including cyberbullying, and let school staff know what steps have already been taken.

### *Technology in schools*

Professor Byron expressed concern that many schools are so concerned with minimizing risk (and thus locking down access to many sites on the internet) that they are not providing an environment that enables children to take responsibility for their own safety:

*Instead it meant that they weren't able to access a range of sites that are beneficial for learning, and that they were less likely to develop the understanding of digital safety that they needed to be digitally safe outside of school.*[4]

The Canadian MediaSmarts Annual Report (2012) noted that many schools are trying to manage risk by capturing everything students do and say in order to maintain control.

In 2010, Sir Ken Robinson, an international education advisor, called for a change in attitude towards schooling, which he said should not be "like making motorcars". Children are individuals; they are not all good at the same things, and they need different learning approaches.[5] Schools are increasingly considering or encouraging "Bring your own devices" (BYOD), in which children bring in their own technology for use in the classroom. Bearing in mind what we said earlier about the impact of the "digital divide", teachers also need to be aware that their "technology-enhanced" teaching practices may have an impact on the ability of some students to partake fully in activities.

· · · · · · · · · · · · · · · · · · · · · · · · · · · · · · · · · · ·

Despite all the advantages of digital communication, it certainly presents parents with more challenges with regard to keeping one's child safe and preserving their innocence, as well as the cost implications. Schools will expect pupils to communicate more and more with teachers and complete homework online. This can be beneficial to both child and parent, but will require a certain level of technology in the home that is accessible to the child.

**(Parent, 2 or under)**

One of the people I most respect for keeping on top of the latest opportunities in education, particularly those provided through technology, is Professor Steve Wheeler, who organizes the Plymouth Enhanced Learning Conference. If you want to read about the latest thinking on technology and schools, check out his website: http://steve-wheeler.blogspot.co.uk.

### Policies and programmes

Schools need to ensure that firm policies are available to allow students to become digitally literate and to ensure their online health and safety. Guidelines are likely to cover acceptable use, including obligations, responsibilities, and consequences of breaking the rules. Suggestions for policies can be found on JISC's e-safety toolkit: http://j.mp/JISCesafety, and further advice can be found on your local "Grid for Learning" (Google that term!).

· · · · · · · · · · · · · · · · · · · · · · · · · · · · · · · · ·

I also think that every school should have to take part in and do something on Safer Internet Day (in February) — this way, at least once a year, children would have access to information and details of how to function in their digital world.
**(Parent, 6 to 9)**

*Find more information on Safer Internet Day at: http://www. saferInternet.org.uk/safer-Internet-day/http://www.saferInternet.org. uk/safer-Internet-day/*

Even more important is a need to create an environment in which parents, teachers, and students (particularly in secondary schools and above) are open to discussing the issues. Students need encouragement to consider what it means to be a good digital citizen, by being accountable for their own actions and also aware and respectful of the feelings of others. Dr Shaheen Shariff's study of cyberbullying noted that autocratic leadership styles lead to student disengagement, boredom, and violence, whereas a more democratic and distributed leadership approach leads to thriving learning and social relationships. Simply writing policies without providing opportunities to discuss them within the curriculum is not enough: the approach that "zero tolerance will frighten young people into treating each other nicely" simply wastes opportunities for dialogue.[6] You could call in someone like Nick Booth, who won the 2012 Big Society Award from the British Prime Minister[7] for the socially entrepreneurial "social media surgeries". If you plan to run something similar in schools, read about their programme and adapt it for your own environment.[8]

Nancy Willard, school cyberbullying expert, suggests a number of strategies for creating effective dialogue, including conducting online surveys of students, asking what behaviour they observe, how they would like peers to behave, and when they would like adult intervention. The results can be shared in class, encouraging students to analyse them and create their own positive statements and policies for use within the school, and opportunities to practise positive engagement. Other opportunities for discussion can be raised in connection with news stories and incidents within the school, and by sharing statistics among peers that demonstrate positive norms, such as "90 per cent of x school students have set their social networking profile to 'friends only'".[9]

Schools can think about providing a Facebook page that parents and children can check regularly for notices, and also consider text-messaging systems for emergencies, including allowing students to text in anonymous queries to teachers trained to respond to concerns such as cyberbullying reports or drugs.

### Protecting yourself as a teacher

At e-learning conferences, there is a lot of discussion of the particular aspects that the digital world raises for teachers, including the kind of relationship that teachers should have with students online. Be aware that you are likely to be "Googled" by your students, so think about the material that you post online. Regarding Facebook, the advice generally is not to be "friends" with students but to create groups or pages. A number of teachers have Facebook accounts under false names, but, as with all interaction online, it should be assumed that at any time these could be made public. It is worth noting that students may also set up false profiles, so be wary about adding strangers to your account, particularly to avoid the dangers of bullying directed at teachers.

With the near-ubiquitous mobile culture, it is likely that students will take photos and record teachers (via video or audio). Schools need to have clear policies on what is permissible with regard to this, and what use can be made of the data collected, and must take the time to discuss it with students and parents.

With regard to sexting, legally there is some important advice to note. If you confiscate a phone and it has an image on it, do not touch the phone: let the police deal with it; otherwise you may be convicted of accessing/sharing child porn. Certainly don't forward the image to yourself to deal with. Expect that everyone involved will be on the defensive.

## Some further resources
- http://www.teachtoday.eu
  Teachtoday was largely developed by a UK team
  to provide information and advice for those in the
  school workforce seeking to understand the positive,
  responsible, and safe use of new technologies.
- http://www.jisclegal.ac.uk/Themes/eSafety.aspx
  Particularly designed for sixth forms and universities, this
  site gives information on a variety of legal matters within
  the e-safety context, including cyberbullying, harassment,
  defamation, hosting liability, and data protection.

- http://www.childnet.com/ufiles/Social-networking.pdf
  Social Networking: A Guide for Trainee Teachers and
  NQTs: useful advice and things to think about as you
  join the classroom.
- http://www.guardian.co.uk/teacher-network
  *The Guardian* Teacher Network provides a range of
  free resources and expert tips for UK teachers, and
  encourages you to upload your own.
- http://www.digizen.org/downloads/cyberbullying_
  teachers.pdf
  Useful guidance provided by the British government
  with support from a range of agencies.
- http://edudemic.com
  A US-based site designed to provide tools, tips, and
  resources for teachers, administrators, and students.
- http://www.ofsted.gov.uk/resources/safe-use-of-new-
  technologies
  A small study from 2009, evaluating the extent to which
  schools taught pupils to adopt safe and responsible
  practices in using new technologies, and how they
  achieved this.

### Youth workers/leaders

Similar advice to that for teachers applies to many in youth
work, including taking particular care over the information you
share online. A 2009 survey emphasized that many in youth
work end up engaging and working with socially excluded
young people and those with complex needs. These groups
may lack access to technology, and are more vulnerable to risks
when they are engaged with online social networking.[10]

Paul Windo, Communications Manager for Urban Saints,
emphasizes that youth leaders have great opportunities to
befriend the young people they work with, and to engage them
in debates about topics such as identity, self-worth, belonging,

and integrity. There are also great opportunities to make use of the tools in a practical way:

• • • • • • • • • • • • • • • • • • • • • • • • • • • • • • • • • • • • •

> For me as a youth leader, it's a very convenient way of messaging and informing members of our youth group, and inviting them to events and [connecting with] each other when we're not together… Sadly, for your child to be the only one in a group NOT to have access to Facebook can itself be a cause of isolation — they may not get invitations to youth events, for example, and be ridiculed and bullied for being the "odd one out".
>
> **(Parent, 16 to 19)**

### Policies and guidelines

Social media need to be considered within overall policy decisions, including developing policies for how youth leaders will deal with pastoral questions and suicidal "cries for help", and providing an easily accessible list of contacts available for staff to use. Again, Paul Windo offers us some advice:

*Permissions/Consent*
- Obtain permission from parents for contacting young people via email, mobile or other platform.
- Establish consent for the use of photographs for publicity, on group websites, or for placing on Facebook.
- Consider devising a catch-all statement to put on registration forms, which assumes these permissions unless parents opt out.

*Language*
- Use clear, unambiguous language, avoiding abbreviations that can be misinterpreted. For example, "LOL" usually means "Laugh Out Loud", but can also be read as "Lots of Love".

- Take care how you sign off in communications. Avoid things such as "luv" and "xxx".

### Protecting yourself as a youth leader
In using communications technology, great care must be taken to ensure that both the young people and the leaders/workers responsible for them are not put at risk and that there are clear boundaries in place and means of accountability provided.

#### Accountability
- Publish and display "guidelines" that both leaders and young people have contributed to – especially where there is unsupervised internet use.
- Be prepared to grant your line manager access to your social networking accounts.
- If you would have a second leader in the room if you were meeting face to face, ensure that others are copied in to emails or Facebook messages.
- Save any potentially abusive emails or disclosures of abuse, either for future reference or to be passed on to the appropriate person.

#### Confidentiality
In digital communications with youth/children, be aware that they may be prepared to disclose more than they would face to face. Ensure that those in your group understand that you are not qualified to provide counselling (unless you are!), but can give general advice in a personal capacity. Consider adding a disclaimer such as the following about what you may do with their information:

*If there is a concern, e.g. that the sender or someone else, particularly a child, may be at risk of serious harm, we may need to share those concerns. In such circumstances we would inform the sender, giving details of who would be contacted and what information would be given.*[11]

*Boundaries*
- Consider having a dedicated mobile phone/social networking page specifically for work that provides more accountable interaction with young people and protects your personal privacy. *Note that Facebook terms and conditions do not allow users to have more than one profile.*
- It's not recommended to keep images of young people on personal devices – these should be downloaded and stored on devices owned by the organization.
- Define curfews for exchanges of instant/direct messaging on social media.

## Some further resources
- http://network.youthworkonline.org.uk
  An online community for debating the impact of digital technologies on work with young people, and the policy or practices of digital youth work.
- http://www.youthworkessentials.org
  Developed by "You Scotland", a set of resources designed to help you develop high-quality and inclusive programmes for young people.
- http://youthworktoolbox.com
  A site set up by a UK practitioner to share advice, guidance, and resources that have all been tested and proved to be effective.
- http://www.cypnow.co.uk/category/disciplines/youth-work
  An offshoot of the magazine designed for professionals working in the sector.

# 17

# Looking to the Future

*The wiser the person thinking about the future of the web,*
*the more likely they are to admit as early as possible that no*
*one really knows what will happen next.*[1]

Futurologists in the 1960s forecast flying cars, jetpacks, hoverboards, inflatable foods, and holidays to the moon for the twenty-first century. Ian Goldin said in a TED talk in 2009: "Our mobile phones are more powerful than the total Apollo space engines."[2] Even ten years before Facebook was created, no one had predicted such a thing, although some are predicting that Facebook's user base will now start to age as younger users seek more intimate experiences.[3] So who can know what is yet to come?

### Predictions are made

There are plenty who are prepared to make predictions, and these tend to focus on faster, smaller devices that are more wearable, with a longer battery life. They also expect that privacy and security will become more and more important for hardware, software, and policy developers to focus on.

In February 2012, the Pew Internet Project published a report entitled "Millennials will benefit and suffer due to their hyperconnected lives", in which a number of leading social media thinkers were asked for their views on what life will be like in 2020. Predictions were wide and varied, and included the ability to share information at speed, ignoring political, geographical, and time borders, with digital assistance provided via cloud-based services. Some are more negative, seeing a world in which presentation and entertainment will win over expertise and substance. Yet others see both positives and negatives as technology becomes so integrated into our lives that it essentially disappears, but those who are able to maintain "the state of being whole and undivided" and are able to think about what they are doing and why they are doing it will be in demand.[4]

Even the "experts" can't agree, so where do we go from here?

**EXERCISE: Have some fun with your child, undertaking some "no-limits futurology". What do they think life will look like in x number of years? Think about creating a "souvenir" book to bring back out at that time in the future.**

### The future is here

Over the past four years I've attended "Thinking Digital", a brain-melting event that gives exposure to lots of new ideas, and aims to inspire those who "want to understand how our future will be affected by technology and other world changing ideas".[5] Some ideas that originally seemed purely futuristic you may have started to hear about, or even seen in daily use, including augmented reality, Google Glasses, Perceptive Radio (which all add digital layers of information to the physical world, adapting to the surrounding environment) and 3D printing (which has started to replace years of mechanical production with digital production).

As things continue to change, it's good to be reminded of these words from Professor Tanya Byron:

*We cannot make the Internet completely safe. Because of this, we must also build children's resilience to the material to which they may be exposed so that they have the confidence and the skills to navigate these new media waters more safely.*[6]

## Core parenting skills retain value

As in the past, both disaster and utopia will be predicted as the result of new technologies. Parents and carers, however, need simply to continue doing a good job, drawing on core parenting skills that have worked for years. These include providing a safe space for children to grow up in and the means to communicate, making the most of the opportunities and resources available, and questioning (and supporting) industry, the government, and educators who provide for them. Most importantly, with regard to technology, stay educated and interested in what your child is learning and doing, and how it is affecting them. Ensure they understand that you are with them on their "digital journey".

# 18

# Never Forget

Remember what this grandmother said:

. . . . . . . . . . . . . . . . . . . . . . . . . . . . . . . . . .

The digital age isn't going to go away, so children
have to be prepared for it.

**(Grandparent, 6 to 9)**

Recollect how we started:

. . . . . . . . . . . . . . . . . . . . . . . . . . . . . . . . . .

Don't be scared, don't be fearful; just be aware and
help your children to navigate this phase of life.

**(Parent, 13 to 15, 16 to 18)**

. . . . . . . . . . . . . . . . . . . . . . . . . . . . . . . . . .

Parents cannot pass this responsibility entirely
to schools; we need to take responsibility too.
Also, debate needs to be balanced and to encourage
good practice — horror stories about sexting, porn
access, and oversexualization can be effective in
raising awareness but they also increase fear in
parents and provoke a desire to operate a blanket
ban rather than a more balanced way forward.

> Technology is here to stay, and we need to find ways of encouraging children to engage with it safely, not simply ban them from it.
>
> **(Parent, 10 to 12)**

Be encouraged that CHILDWISE surveys have demonstrated that children's loyalty continues to be to their friends rather than to any specific platform, and they would move social networks if necessary. They are less concerned with technological developments than with those things that affect their lives directly.

I spotted this on Facebook as I was coming to the end of writing this book. It was posted by Will Taylor (communications manager, youth worker, and dad), and seems to sum up what is required of parents in the digital sphere:

- Do it for them.
- Do it with them.
- Watch while they do it.
- Let them do it for themselves.

As this parent puts it:

· · · · · · · · · · · · · · · · · · · · · · · · · · · · · · · · · · ·

> Supervision is very important at a younger age: as the child gets older they need to make more decisions themselves but with the information you have discussed; you need to trust that they will make the right choices.
>
> **(Parent, 16 to 18, 19 or over)**

Finally, I'll leave it to one of the parents who responded to my questionnaire to have the last word, as it sums up much of what this book has been about:

Parents *have* to be actively involved in their children's online life. It's not a privacy issue, it's a parenting one. We have to keep them safe, teach them to manage themselves in a safely controlled environment, and be smartly aware of the culture they are a part of. Young people are biologically hindered from making wise decisions… they need to be nurtured, encouraged, supported, and kept safe, in the real and virtual worlds. We have to get beyond the notion that because they LOOK as if they are grown up, they are capable of managing their lives in an adult way. I have observed that my daughter needs me more now as a teenager than she did as a toddler… the needs are different, but, if anything, far more serious. She deserves my input, guidance, and protection, and I haven't come this far in her life to abandon her now.

**(Parent, 13 to 15) 16**

# JargonBuster

The terminology can seem intimidating, but there's no need for it to be – there's a huge range of online sites that will help you keep up with the latest terminology, but first of all let's give you a taster of some useful terms.

### Access control/Filter
A bar that is put in place by (e.g.) an internet or mobile provider to prevent access to certain content.

### Application (App)
A piece of software, often designed to run on smartphones and other devices.

### BBM (BlackBerry Messenger)
A free instant-messaging app, popular because large bills are not run up. On devices other than BlackBerry from summer 2013.

### Bluetooth
A way of exchanging data over short distances between mobile devices.

### Browser
A software program used to display webpages, including Internet Explorer, Google Chrome, Safari, and Firefox.

### Cloud computing
Also known as "the cloud", this allows users to access their data from anywhere rather than being tied to a particular machine.

### Cookie
A piece of text stored on your computer by a web browser that remembers information about you, such as websites you've visited.

**Creative Commons**

Licences that allow creators to give the public permission to share and use creative work. Six different licences exist, at the heart of which all users must acknowledge the creator as the originator of the work.

**Creeping**

Similar to stalking in the physical world, following what is going on in someone's life by watching their status messages and social networking updates to an unhealthy degree.

**Crowdsourcing**

Refers to outsourcing tasks, encouraging volunteers to contribute their time, skills, and content in problem solving. Wikipedia is a crowdsourced encyclopaedia.

**Cyberlocker**

File-hosting and file-sharing services, typically used for documents, music, and other large files.

**Digital footprint**

The digital trail left by all your online activities and interactions, such as emails, web searches, uploaded photos, and text messages. Sometimes the terms "digital fingerprint" (your unique impression online) and "digital shadow" (more sinister) are used.

**Drag and drop**

Where a virtual object is selected and moved to a different location, usually with a simple mouse-click.

**Drama**

Most commonly characterized by interactions between teenage girls, involving backstabbing, blackmailing, gossiping and betraying friends, but often falling short of "bullying" as defined by power imbalances.

**Embedding**

Code added to a website to display a video or photo, while the original is hosted on another site, such as YouTube or Flickr.

**Flashmob**

A group of people who assemble suddenly in a public place, perform an unusual and seemingly pointless act for a brief time, and then quickly disperse. Often used for fun, artistic expression, or advertising.

**Geotag**

Where location-identification data is added to media such as photos, videos or online messages via a GPS device, such as a smartphone.

**GPS**

Short for Global Positioning System, a navigation satellite system. GPS-enabled devices support precise pinpointing of the location of people, buildings, and objects.

**Hashtag**

Originating from Twitter but used more widely, a hashtag is community-defined and functions as an "index", allowing users to aggregate, organize, and discover relevant posts.

**Hosting**

Hosting services are provided by companies that sell space on servers, allowing webpages to appear live on the World Wide Web.

**Hyper-local**

Making use of digital technology to augment the experiences of living in a geographical community.

**IMEI (International Mobile Equipment Identity)**

A unique identifying number on your mobile, usually printed inside the battery compartment.

**In-app purchase**

Once you've downloaded an app, you can purchase additional content and features, such as new outfits or abilities for a character in the game, and tokens that allow you to skip levels. Usually small amounts, but they can add up.

**Instant Messaging (IM)**

A form of real-time communication between two or more people, based on typed text and undertaken on the internet.

**IP address (Internet Protocol address)**

A unique number that identifies every computer on the internet.

**Lifecasting**

An around-the-clock broadcast of events in a person's life through digital media, often involving wearable technology.

**Malware**

Malicious software, such as viruses and worms, which infiltrates and damages computers.

**Mashup**

Combining two or more pieces of data (music, video, program) to create a new work.

**Meme**

An often humorous concept that evolves and spreads rapidly from person to person via the internet, frequently in video or image form, typically drawing on popular cultural references. *Keep Calm and Have a Cup of Tea*, anyone?

**Metadata**

Data that describes other data, such as titles, descriptions, tags, and captions, attached to internet files such as videos, photos or blog posts, to enable easier searching and discovery.

**MP3**

A common format for digital music files, compressing data to make the file smaller and easier to download.

### Open source

Originally defining software code that is free for others to develop, build upon, and share, open source now refers to the practice of collaboration and free sharing of media and information for the benefit of the global community.

### Peer-to-Peer (P2P)

Most commonly understood as a network on which users can share files, such as music.

### Phishing

Unsolicited emails or texts, often from someone claiming to be e.g. a bank, sent in an attempt to get personal information such as passwords and credit card details from you.

### Plug-in

A set of software components built into a larger software application, allowing the handling of particular types of data, such as video in a web browser.

### Podcast

A podcast is a digital file (usually audio but sometimes video) made available for download to a portable device or personal computer for later playback, sometimes individually, sometimes as a series.

### Rogue app

A piece of malicious software disguised as a mobile web application, used to harvest your personal data, or spam other users.

### RSS feed

Short for Really Simple Syndication, this enables users to sign up to a blog and be alerted to new content via email or a newsreader, without having to go back to the original site. All blogs, podcasts, and video feeds have RSS feeds.

### Screencast

A screencast is a video that captures what takes place on a computer screen, usually accompanied by audio narration, often used in "how to" videos.

### Selfie

A carefully posed picture taken of yourself, designed for a social networking website, often taken in a mirror, or with a visible arm holding the camera.

### Sexting

A blend of sex and texting: the act of sending sexually explicit messages and/or photographs, predominantly between mobile phones but also on other digital devices.

### Spam

Unsolicited email or text messages, often advertising, sent indiscriminately to large numbers of users.

### Spyware

Software that gathers information about you and your online habits without your knowledge. Used "legitimately" to give you content you may be interested in, it can also be used maliciously for more nefarious purposes.

### Streaming media

Refers to video or audio that can be watched or listened to online but not downloaded or stored permanently.

### Tablet

A single-screen mobile computer, larger than a phone, such as the iPad, Nexus 7 and Samsung Galaxy Tab.

### Tag

A way of assigning a piece of information or an image to a particular person (including Facebook photos), helping to describe an item and allowing it to be found again by browsing or searching.

**Terms of Service**

Sometimes shortened to TOS, these are the legal basis upon which you agree to use a website, video hosting site or other place for creating or sharing content. Check whether you are giving away rights to your content before agreeing.

**Troll**

Someone who posts controversial, inflammatory, irrelevant or off-topic messages to an online community, with the intention of provoking other users to respond emotionally or disrupting normal on-topic discussion.

**UGC**

Short for user-generated content, an industry term that refers to all forms of user-created (rather than paid-creation) materials, such as blog posts, reviews, podcasts, videos, comments, and more.

**Virtual world**

An online computer-simulated environment that allows users to interact with each other through a representation of themselves (an avatar), and use and create objects within that space. Typically referring to interactive 3D virtual spaces, Second Life is still one of the best known of these.

**Wi-Fi**

Allows enabled devices to connect to the internet within short range of any access point without cables or adaptors.

## Find other terms

Recommendations for further help include:

- http://www.socialbrite.org/sharing-center/glossary/
- http://www.teachtoday.eu/en/Technology-today/Jargon-Buster.aspx
- http://www.techopedia.com/it-dictionary
- http://www.urbandictionary.com
- http://www.w3schools.com/web/web_glossary.asp
- http://www.webopedia.com

# Websites You Might Want to Connect with

. . . . . . . . . . . . . . . . . . . . . . . . . . . . . . . . .

Computers are all in the living room, permission
is required to use them, and we limit their time on
them. We discuss what sites they can or can't use.
Sites are monitored by checking browser history
if we suspect they've not done as they're told.
Email they send is forwarded to one of our accounts
and we supervise them when using email. I'm a
CEOP ambassador and all my children have used the
thinkuknow website and have a good understanding of
Internet safety.

**(Parent, 3 to 5, 6 to 9, 10 to 12)**

There's certainly no shortage of websites designed to help
parents gain confidence (with their children) online. Here we
pick out some of the best:

**www.bbc.co.uk/webwise/**

A range of information, news stories, and links to TV programmes, provided by
the BBC and including advice specifically for parents: http://www.bbc.co.uk/
webwise/0/21259412, which contains information on how to set parental
controls on video-on-demand services.

**www.bullying.org**

Defined as "the world's most-visited and referenced website about bullying",
based in Canada, this website is keen to support individuals and organizations
in taking positive actions against, and finding non-violent solutions to,
bullying through the sharing of resources. It provides the website: http://www.
cyberbullying.org.

## Raising Children in a Digital Age

### www.childline.org.uk/explore/

ChildLine's website has a section designed for children and young people to help with a range of online matters, including sexting, mobile safety, online gaming, privacy, and cyberbullying.

### www.childnet.org

Childnet International works in partnership with other organizations to help make the internet a safe place for children and young people, drawing upon real children's experiences. Information is provided for parents, carers, teachers, and professionals. It also provides further resources on "Know It All" and www.chatdanger.com/.

### www.childwise.co.uk

CHILDWISE have conducted research into children, young people, and their families since 1991. They produce an annual "Monitor Report", focusing on children and young people's media consumption, brand attitudes, and behaviours, as well as Special Reports including "Digital Lives" in 2010.

### www.youtube.com/user/CommonSenseMedia

YouTube channel including movie reviews (US-based) and tips for parents raising children in the digital age, plus useful videos to discuss with your children.

### www.connectsafely.org

A US-based site designed to help parents, teens, educators, advocates, and policy makers learn about safe, civil use of web and mobile technology.

### www.cybersmart.gov.au

Cybersmart provides educational materials for an Australian audience, designed to empower children to be safe online, with material specifically for children, young people, parents, teachers, and library staff.

### www.digitalme.co.uk

Aimed particularly at educators, DigitalMe is designed to help young people gain skills and confidence through new technology.

### www.digizen.org

"Digital citizenship" is about building safe spaces and communities, becoming a responsible digital citizen, and thinking about how your own behaviour online affects your own and others' online experiences. There are sections specifically for teachers, parents, and children.

### https://www.education.gov.uk/childrenandyoungpeople/safeguarding children/b00222029/child-internet-safety

Advice on safeguarding from the Department for Education, including links to a number of useful resources.

### www.fosi.org

An international, non-profit organization, encouraging debate and innovation to make the online world safer for children and their families. It seeks to promote a culture of responsibility online, encouraging a sense of digital citizenship for all. It was established in 1996 by the internet industry to allow the UK public to report criminal online content securely and confidentially.

### www.huffingtonpost.com/news/parents-families-tech

A news site that posts interesting, entertaining, and not-too-scaremongering stories about technology and the family.

### kidsblogclub.com

A site for children who blog and their parents to gain information, inspiration, and support, founded by a UK-based author, journalist, and blogging mum, with her two blogging children.

### www.kidscape.org.uk

Kidscape has a range of information for both children and adults, with some interactive sections for children and young people on responding to bullying.

### blog.kidzvuz.com

A site designed for "tweens" and their parents, focusing on children's entertainment, books, and new media.

### www.mashable.com

Mashable is one of the leading web sources for information on social media, and regularly posts stories about technological developments, research, and apps related to children. Includes the category: http://mashable.com/category/family-parenting/

### www.microsoft.com/security/default.aspx

Microsoft's security and safety site, including practical advice on how to set up your Microsoft computer safely.

### www.mumsnet.com/Internet-safety

A space for parents to share hints, tips, and stories, and access information to protect children online and on mobile devices.

### www.netfamilynews.org

Written by parents for parents, designed as a public service, "based on the premise that informed, engaged parenting is essential to children's constructive use of technology", supported by a filtering software company.

### www.netsafe.org.nz/

Designed for the New Zealand audience, NetSafe is an independent non-profit organization promoting confident, safe, and responsible use of online technologies.

### www.netsmartz.org/Parents

Another American site, with materials for parents, age-grouped children, teachers, and the law, with a range of profiles and interactive material. Comes from a "risk" perspective.

### stakeholders.ofcom.org.uk/market-data-research/media-literacy-pubs/

Research by Ofcom into the media literacy of children and adults in the UK.

### www.theparentzone.co.uk/

A site designed to help facilitate parents, as the experts, supporting and engaging others to help meet parents' needs.

### www.pewInternet.org

The Pew Internet & American Life Project produces reports exploring the impact of the internet on families, communities, work and home, daily life, education, health care, and civic and political life, affecting both America and the world.

### www.respectme.org.uk

Funded by the Scottish government, the respectme website offers practical advice and guidance for adults on addressing bullying behaviour. There are sections that specifically offer practical advice and guidance for professionals, parents, and children and young people who are being bullied.

### www.thinkuknow.co.uk

Run by the team at the Child Exploitation and Online Protection (CEOP) Centre, information is provided for children and youth by age about the websites they like to visit, mobiles, and new technology. Sections are also provided for parents, carers, and teachers.

### www.vodafone.com/parents/

Vodafone launched the Digital Parenting website in 2009 in order to help parents feel more confident about getting involved in and setting boundaries for their child's digital world.

### www.youngandwellcrc.org.au

An Australian research organization focusing on technology and young people's mental health and well-being, encouraging cyber safety, resilience, and creativity. Includes the "Keep It Tame" initiative: http://keepittame. youngandwellcrc.org.au/.

# Want to Read a Little More?

If you're interested in reading more about some of the topics covered in this book, below are some suggestions, including a number that were drawn on for research for the book:

Anderson, J., *Cyberbullying: The Truth Behind the Shocking New Internet Trends*, Amazon, 2012.

Anderson, J., *Bully Defense: Don't Be a Target*, Amazon, 2012.

Bair, A. L., *Raising Digital Families for Dummies*, For Dummies, 2013.

Bazelon, E., *Sticks and Stones: Defeating the Culture of Bullying and Rediscovering the Power of Character and Empathy*, Random House, 2013.

Buckingham, D., *Beyond Technology: Children's Learning in the Age of Digital Culture*, Polity, 2007.

Buckingham, D., *Youth, Identity & Digital Culture*, MIT Press, 2008.

Burrows, T., *Blogs, Wikis, Facebook and More: Everything You Want to Know about Using Today's Internet But Are Afraid to Ask*, Carlton, 2011.

Carr, N., *The Shallows: How the Internet is Changing the Way We Think, Read and Remember*, Atlantic Books, 2011.

Carr-Gregg, M., *Real Wired Child: What Parents Need to Know about Kids Online*, Penguin Books, 2007.

Chatfield, T., *How to Thrive in the Digital Age*, Macmillan, 2012.

Clark, L. S., *The Parent App: Understanding Families in the Digital Age*, OUP USA, 2012.

Davies, C. and Eynon, R., *Teenagers and Technology*, Routledge, 2013.

Dutwin, D., *Unplug Your Kids: A Parent's Guide to Raising Happy, Active and Well-Adjusted Children in the Digital Age*, Adams Media Corporation, 2009.

Edgington, S. M., *The Parent's Guide to Texting, Facebook, and Social Media: Understanding the Benefits and Dangers of Parenting in a Digital World*, Brown Books, 2011.

Facer, K., *Learning Futures: Education, Technology and Social Change*, Routledge, 2011.

Furedi, F., *Paranoid Parenting: Why Ignoring the Experts May be Best for Your Child*, A Capella, 2002.

Gardner, D., *Risk: The Science and Politics of Fear*, Virgin Books, 2009

Guerry, R., *Public and Permanent: Creating a Mindset That Our Digital Actions Are Public and Permanent*, Youthlight, 2013.

Harkin, J., *Cyburbia: The Dangerous Idea That's Changing How We Live and Who We Are*, Little, Brown, 2009.

Harris, F. J., *I found it on the Internet*, American Library Association, 2011.

Henderson, L., *Darknet: A Beginners Guide to Staying Anonymous Online*, Lance Henderson, 2012.

Holloway, S. L. and Valentine, G., *Cyberkids: Children in the Information Age*, Routledge, 2003.

Jarvis, J., *What Would Google Do?*, Harper Collins, 2011.

Jones, R. H. and Hafner, C. A., *Understanding Digital Literacies: A Practical Introduction*, Routledge, 2012.

Krotoski, A., *Untangling the Web: What the Internet is doing to YOU*, Faber & Faber, 2013.

Leaning, M., *The Internet, Power and Society: Rethinking the Power of the Internet to Change Lives*, Chandos, 2009.

Livingstone, S., *Children and the Internet: Great Expectations, Challenging Realities*, Polity, 2009.

Livingstone, S., Haddon, L., and Gorzig, A., *Children, Risk and Safety on the Internet: Research and Policy Challenges in Comparative Perspective*, Polity Press, 2012.

Loos, E., Haddon, L. and Mante-Meijer, E., *Generational Use of New Media*, Ashgate, 2012.

Mayfield, A., *Me and My Web Shadow*, A&C Black, 2010.

Mizuko, I. *et al.*, *Hanging Out, Messing Around, and Geeking Out*, MIT Press, 2009.

O'Keeffe, G. S., *CyberSafe: Protecting and Empowering Kids in the Digital World of Texting, Gaming and Social Media*, American Academy of Pediatrics, 2011.

Ribble, M., *Raising a Digital Child: A Digital Citizenship Handbook for Parents*, International Society for Technology in Education, 2009.

Rosner, M., *Digital Manners & House Rules for Kids: A Parent Handbook*, Amazon, 2010.

Shariff, S. and Churchill, A. H., *Truths and Myths of Cyber-bullying: International Perspectives on Stakeholder Responsibility and Children's Safety*, Peter Lang Publishing, 2009.

Stephens, K. and Nair, V., *Cyberslammed: A Digital Pile On*, Smashup Press, 2013.

Stanko, D., *Digital Danger: If You Think Your Kid is Safe Online, Think Again*, CreateSpace Independent Publishing Platform, 2013.

Steyer, J. P., *The Other Parent: The Inside Story of the Media's Effect on Our Children*, Atria, 2003.

Tapscott, D., *Grown-Up Digital: How the Net Generation is Changing Your World*, 2008.

Taylor, J., *Raising Generation Tech: Preparing Your Children for a Media-Fuelled World*, 2012 .

Trolley, B. C. and Hanel, C., *Cyberkids, Cyber Bullying, Cyber Balance*, Corwin, 2010.

Turkle, S., *Alone Together: Why We Expect More From Technology, and Less From Each Other*, 2011.

Vandome, N., *A Parent's Guide to the iPad*, Easy Steps, 2012.

Whitby, P., *Is Your Child Safe Online: A Parents Guide to the Internet, Facebook, Mobile Phones & Other New Media*, Crimson, 2011.

Willard, N., *Cyber-Savvy: Embracing Digital Safety and Civility*, Corwin, 2012.

## Some specific web resources

ACMA (Australian Communications and Media Authority) "Click and connect: Young Australians' use of online social media", 2009, http://www.acma.gov.au/webwr/aba/about/recruitment/click_and_connect-01_qualitative_report.pdf

Anderson, J. and Rainie, L. "Millennials will benefit and suffer due to their hyperconnected lives", Pew Internet, February 2012, http://pewInternet.org/Reports/2012/Hyperconnected-lives.aspx

Byron, T., The Byron Reviews, UKCCIS, 2008/2010, http://www.education.gov.uk/ukccis/about/a0076277/the-byron-reviews

Common Sense Media, "Teens and Their Digital Life", 2012, http://www.commonsensemedia.org/sites/default/files/research/socialmediasociallife-final-061812.pdf

Dutton, W. H. and Blank, G., "Next Generation Users: The Internet in Britain", Oxford Internet Survey, 2011, http://www.oii.ox.ac.uk/publications/oxis2011_report.pdf

Gilkerton, L., "Parenting the Internet Generation: 7 Potential Threats and 7 Habits for Internet Safety", http://www.covenanteyes.com/parenting-the-internet-generation, 2012

Kang, C., "Preteens' use of Instagram", Pew Internet, May 2013, http://www.pewInternet.org/Media-Mentions/2013/Preteens-use-of-Instagram-creates-privacy-issue-child-advocates-say.aspx

Kerr, J. C., "Poll: Teens Migrating to Twitter", Pew Internet, May 2013, http://www.pewInternet.org/Media-Mentions/2013/Poll-Teens-migrating-to-Twitter.aspx

Leggat, S., "Children and their media 2013", CHILDWISE, 2013, http://prezi.com/6spkttfivlhp/children-and-their-media-2013/

Ofcom, "Children and Parents: Media Use and Attitudes Report", Ofcom, 2012, http://stakeholders.ofcom.org.uk/binaries/research/media-literacy/oct2012/main.pdf

Ofcom, "The Reinvention of the 1950s Living Room", Ofcom, 2013, http://media.ofcom.org.uk/2013/08/01/the-reinvention-of-the-1950s-living-room-2/

UKCCIS, "Good Practice Guidance for the Moderation of Interactive Services for Children", 2010, http://dera.ioe.ac.uk/1969/1/industry%20guidance%20%20%20moderation.pdf

Urban Saints, "Totally Wired – The 2012 Tour", 2012, http://vimeo.com/51279921

# Notes

## Introduction

1. "The Byron Reviews", linked from Child Internet Safety, Department for Education, http://www.education.gov.uk/childrenandyoungpeople/ safeguardingchildren/b00222029/child-internet-safety (2008/2010).

2. CHILDWISE, "Digital Lives Report", 2010.

3. Whitby, P., *Is Your Child Safe Online? A Parent's Guide to the Internet, Facebook, Mobile Phones & Other New Media*, Crimson, 2011, p. 7

4. Gardner, D., *Risk: The Science and Politics of Fear*, Virgin Books, 2009, p. 15.

5. "Don't Fear Your Kids' Technology Use; Embrace It", Rebecca Levey, http://mashable.com/2013/03/22/embracing-kids-technology, 23/3/13.

6. Mayfield, A., *Me and My Web Shadow*, Bloomsbury Publishing, 2010, p. 10.

7. "Questionnaire: #Digital Parenting", Digital Fingerprint, http://digital-fingerprint.co.uk/2013/02/questionnaire-digitalparenting, 4/2/13.

## Chapter 1

1. "Digital Skills as Important as Numeracy and Literacy", Wales Online, http://www.walesonline.co.uk/news/wales-news/digital-skills-important-numeracy-literacy-4005887, 23/5/13.

2. Leaning, M., *The Internet, Power and Society: Rethinking the Power of the Internet to Change Lives*, Chandos, 2009, p. 1.

3. Gardner, D., *Risk: The Science and Politics of Fear*, Virgin Books, 2009, p. 11.

4. Willard, N., *Cyber-Savvy: Embracing Digital Safety and Civility*, Corwin, 2012, p. 29.

5. "Imagining the Internet: Millennials will benefit and suffer due to their hyperconnected lives", Pew Research Center, http://www.pewinternet.org/~/ media//Files/Reports/2012/PIP_Future_of_Internet_2012_Young_brains_PDF. pdf, 29/2/12.

6. Gardner, D., *Risk: The Science and Politics of Fear*, Virgin Books, 2009, pp. 1–4.

7. Gardner, D., *Risk: The Science and Politics of Fear*, Virgin Books, 2009, p. 7.

8. "The Touch-Screen Generation", Hanna Rosin, http://m.theatlantic.com/ magazine/archive/2013/04/the-touch-screen-generation/309250, 20/3/13.

9. "Young Canadians in a Wired World III: Talking to Youth and Parents

about Life Online", MediaSmarts, http://mediasmarts.ca/sites/default/files/pdfs/publication-report/full/YCWWIII-youth-parents.pdf, 2012.

10. "The Acronym Every Parent Should Know: COPPA", Everloop, http://www.everloop.com/the-acronym-every-parent-should-know-coppa, 2013.

11. *Digital Parenting*: Issue 1, Vodafone, http://www.vodafone.com/content/parents/digital-parenting/view_all_magazines.html (November 2010).

12. "Anxiety: The Busy Trap", Tim Kreider, *The New York Times*, http://query.nytimes.com/gst/fullpage.html?res=940DEED8113AF932A35754C0A9649D8B63, 01/07/12.

13. EU Kids Online, London School of Economics, http://www.lse.ac.uk/media@lse/research/EUKidsOnline/Home.aspx

14. "How Technology has made me a better Mom", Jeana Lee Tahnk, http://mashable.com/2013/04/26/technology-better-mom, 26/4/13.

# Chapter 2

1. *Digital Parenting*: Issue 1, Vodafone, http://www.vodafone.com/content/parents/digital-parenting/view_all_magazines.html (November 2010).

2. "Social Media Video 2013", Erik Qualman, http://www.socialnomics.net/2013/01/01/social-media-video-2013, 01/01/13.

3. Clark, L. S., *The Parent App: Understanding Families in the Digital Age*, OUP USA, 2012 and Willard, N., *Cyber-Savvy: Embracing Digital Safety and Civility*, Corwin, 2012, p. 6.

4. "Developing Digital Literacies", JISC, http://www.jisc.ac.uk/whatwedo/programmes/elearning/developingdigitalliteracies.aspx, 01/07/11.

5. "Is technology to blame for the London riots?", Iain McKenzie, http://www.bbc.co.uk/news/technology-14442203, 08/08/11.

6. Clark, L. S., *The Parent App: Understanding Families in the Digital Age*, OUP USA, 2012.

7. "Imagining the Internet: Millennials will benefit and suffer due to their hyperconnected lives", Pew Research Center, http://www.pewinternet.org/~/media//Files/Reports/2012/PIP_Future_of_Internet_2012_Young_brains_PDF.pdf, 29/2/12.

8. "I 'voted' on Facebook", Digital Fingerprint, http://digital-fingerprint.co.uk/2010/05/i-voted-on-faceboo, 06/05/10.

9. "Social Media, Social Lives: How Teenagers View Their Digital Lives", *Common Sense Media*, http://www.commonsensemedia.org/sites/default/files/research/socialmediasociallife-final-061812.pdf, Summer 2012.

10. "Managing social networking for children", *The Daily Telegraph*, http://bundlr.com/clips/514f00bd7461b93d9600006a, April 2013.

11. Sherry Turkle, *Life on the Screen: Identity in the Age of the Internet*, 2005, quoted in Trolley, B. C. and Hanel, C., *Cyberkids, Cyber Bullying, Cyber Balance*, Corwin, 2010.

12. "Next Generation Users: The Internet in Britain 2011", Dutton, W. H. and Blank, G., http://microsites.oii.ox.ac.uk/oxis, Oxford Internet Institute, University of Oxford, 2011.

13. "What is autism?", The National Autistic Society, http://www.autism.org.uk/about-autism/autism-and-asperger-syndrome-an-introduction/what-is-autism.aspx, 27/3/13.

14. Quoted in Whitby, P., *Is Your Child Safe Online: A Parents Guide to the Internet, Facebook, Mobile Phones and Other New Media*, Crimson, 2011, p. 35.

15. Chatfield, T., *How to Thrive in a Digital Age*.

16. "Community", Wikipedia, http://en.wikipedia.org/wiki/Community

17. Mayfield, A., *Me and My Web Shadow*, A & C Black, 2010, p. xix.

# Chapter 3

1. "Don't Fear Your Kids' Technology Use; Embrace It", Rebecca Levey, http://mashable.com/2013/03/22/embracing-kids-technology, 23/3/13.

2. "Children and Their Media 2013", Simon Leggett, CHILDWISE, http://prezi.com/6spkttfivlhp/children-and-their-media-2013/, 2013.

3. "Teens, Social Media, and Privacy", The Pew Research Center, http://www.pewinternet.org/Press-Releases/2013/Teens-Social-Media-and-Privacy.aspx, 21/5/13. See also: "I'm 13 and None of my Friends Use Facebook", Ruby Karp, *Mashable*, http://mashable.com/2013/08/11/teens-Facebook, 11/8/13.

4. http://neverseconds.blogspot.co.uk

5. David Buckingham, *Youth, Identity and Digital Media*, MIT, 2008, pp. 28–30.

6. "How to Convince Your Parents to Let You Get a Facebook Account", WikiHow, http://www.wikihow.com/Convince-Your-Parents-to-Let-You-Get-a-Facebook-Account

7. "Teens, Social Media and Privacy", The Pew Research Center, http://www.pewinternet.org/Press-Releases/2013/Teens-Social-Media-and-Privacy.aspx, 21/5/13.

# Chapter 4

1. "British children online 'for 100 minutes a day'", Alice Philipson, *The Daily Telegraph*, http://www.telegraph.co.uk/technology/news/9611205/British-children-online-for-100-minutes-a-day.html, 16/10/12.

2. "Children and Parents: Media Use and Attitudes Report", Ofcom, http://stakeholders.ofcom.org.uk/binaries/research/media-literacy/oct2012/main.pdf, 23/10/12.

3. "The Web Behaviour Test", BBC, http://www.bbc.co.uk/labuk/articles/webbehaviour/eightanimals.html, January 2010.

4. "Introverts – Extroverts", Ilene Dawn, http://uminntilt.wordpress.com/2013/03/05/introverts-extroverts-change-takes-courage, 05/03/13.

5. "EU Kids Online II (2009–2011)", London School of Economics, http://www.lse.ac.uk/media@lse/research/EUKidsOnline/EU%20Kids%20II%20(2009-11)/home.aspx

6. "Visitors and Residents: A Typology for Online Engagement", David S. White and Alison Le Cornu, *First Monday*, http://firstmonday.org/ojs/index.php/fm/article/view/3171/3049 , Vol. 16:9, 05/09/11.

7. Willard, N., *Cyber-Savvy: Embracing Digital Safety and Civility*, Corwin, 2012, p. vii.

8. "Video-sharing sites top the ranking of risky online platforms for children", EU Kids Online III, London School of Economics, http://www.lse.ac.uk/media@lse/research/EUKidsOnline/EU%20Kids%20III/Press%20releases/IntheirownwordsUKPressRelease.pdf, 05/02/13.

9. http://www.wired.com/magazine/2013/04/genwired/

10. "The Average Teenager Sends 3,339 Texts Per Month", Ben Parr, http://mashable.com/2010/10/14/nielsen-texting-stats, 14/10/10.

11. Jarvis, J., *What Would Google Do?*, HarperCollins, 2011, p. 86.

12. "Good practice guidance for the moderation of interactive services for children", UK Council for Child Internet Safety, http://dera.ioe.ac.uk/1969/1/industry%20guidance%20%20%20moderation.pdf, 2010.

13. Davies, C. and Eynon, R., *Teenagers and Technology*, Routledge, 2013, p. 15.

14. Davies, C. and Eynon, R., *Teenagers and Technology*, Routledge, 2013, p. 57.

15. Davies, C. and Eynon, R., *Teenagers and Technology*, Routledge, 2013, p. 61.

16. Davies, C. and Eynon, R., *Teenagers and Technology*, Routledge, 2013, p. 131. See "Social Scientists Might Gain Access to Facebook's Data on User Behavior", http://www.scientificamerican.com/article.cfm?id=social-scientists-might-gain-access-facebooks-data-user-behavior, July 2012, regarding the restrictions on access to data.

17. "Letting Children Be Children: Report of an Independent Review of the Commercialisation and Sexualisation of Childhood", Reg Bailey, Department for Education, https://www.gov.uk/government/uploads/system/uploads/attachment_data/file/175418/Bailey_Review.pdf, June 2011.

18. "Fake Facebook pages promise free gifts in exchange for 'Likes'", Stephen Musil, *CNet News*, http://news.cnet.com/8301-1023_3-57573495-93/fake-facebook-pages-promise-free-gifts-in-exchange-for-likes, 10/3/13.

19. "Online Shopping", Vodafone, http://www.vodafone.com/content/parents/get-involved/online_shopping.html

20. "How to Teach Kids About Finance – Show Them the Virtual Money", Dan Tynan, *Mashable*, http://mashable.com/2013/03/29/kids-money, 29/3/13.

21. "Give pocket money as pay, otherwise you're 'trust fund teaching'", Martin Lewis, *MoneySavingExpert.com*, http://blog.moneysavingexpert.com/2010/03/05/give-pocket-money-as-pay-otherwise-youre-trust-fund-teaching, 05/03/10.

22. "David Cameron confirms financial education in schools", Helen Knapman, *MoneySavingExpert.com*, http://www.moneysavingexpert.com/news/banking/2013/07/david-cameron-confirms-financial-education-in-schools, 08/07/13. See also a *Guardian* article which raises some useful questions (and answers) for parents to think about in the digital age: "Should kids get digital pocket money?", Stuart Dredge, *The Guardian*, http://www.guardian.co.uk/technology/appsblog/2013/jan/03/kids-digital-pocket-money, 03/01/13.

23. Davies, C. and Eynon, R., *Teenagers and Technology*, Routledge, 2013, p. 103.

24. "EU Kids Online II (2009–2011)", London School of Economics, http://www.lse.ac.uk/media@lse/research/EUKidsOnline/EU%20Kids%20II%20(2009-11)/home.aspx

## Chapter 5

1. "Bad Things Happen to Good Parents: Digital Parenting Tips", Tony Loftis, *The Huffington Post*, http://www.huffingtonpost.com/tony-loftis/digital-parenting-tips_b_2946396.html, 26/03/13.

2. "The Key to Digital Teen Safety: Parental Engagement", Tony Loftis, *The Huffington Post*, http://www.huffingtonpost.com/tony-loftis/the-key-to-digital-teen-s_b_2997251.html, 02/04/13.

3. "ParentPort", UK Media Regulators, http://www.parentport.org.uk

4. Steyer, J. P., *The Other Parent: The Inside Story of the Media's Effect on Our Children*, Atria, 2003, pp. 251–252.

5. "Teach Your Kids How Not to Get Mugged in Minecraft", Beth Blecherman, *Mashable*, http://mashable.com/2013/04/05/kids-tech-talk, 05/04/13.

6. "Expert View: Setting Boundaries", Carrie Longton, Vodafone, http://www.vodafone.com/content/parents/expert-views/setting_boundaries.html

## Chapter 6

1. "Parents' views on parental controls: Findings of qualitative research", Jigsaw Research, http://stakeholders.ofcom.org.uk/binaries/research/media-literacy/oct2012/Annex_1.pdf, October 2012.

2. "Click Clever, Click Safe – help your child enjoy the internet safely", UK government, http://www.nidirect.gov.uk/click-clever-click-safe-help-your-child-enjoy-the-internet-safely, December 2009.

3. "NeverSeconds", Martha Payne, http://neverseconds.blogspot.co.uk/

4. "Kid Tips: Martha Payne On Exploring the Wonderful World of the Web", *ThePositive.com*, http://thepositive.com/kid-tips-martha-payne-on-exploring-the-wonderful-world-of-the-web/, Undated.

5. See: http://www.google.co.uk/url?sa=t&rct=j&q=&esrc=s&source=web&cd=1&ved=0CC4QFjAA&url=http%3A%2F%2Fmelissacanterictportfolio.wikispaces.com%2Ffile%2Fview%2FSafer%2BChildren%2Bin%2Ba

%2BDigital%2BWorld%2BNotes.doc&ei=23V2UpPGAsqu0QWsn4DgAw
&usg=AFQjCNHc7axlOMx9sfGLDEccddxy2j-Iqw&sig2=oqsQFfl4RTk8z-
8CwfJTQw&bvm=bv.55819444,d.d2k, which appear to be notes in
preparation for the report – p. 10.

6. "Facebook admits it is powerless to stop young users setting up profiles",
Mark Sweney, *The Guardian*, http://www.guardian.co.uk/technology/2013/
jan/23/facebook-admits-powerless-young-users, 23/01/13.

7. "Facebook's Zuckerberg Says Privacy No Longer A 'Social Norm'", *The
Huffington Post*, http://www.huffingtonpost.com/2010/01/11/facebooks-
zuckerberg-th'e_n_417969.html, 18/03/10.

8. "Randi Zuckerberg Is Just As Confused By Facebook Privacy As You Are",
Mario Aguilar, *Gizmodo*, http://www.gizmodo.com.au/2012/12/randi-
zuckerberg-is-just-as-confused-by-facebook-privacy-as-you-are, 27/12/12.

9. "Facebook Privacy Settings: Who Cares?", danah boyd and Eszter Hargittai,
*First Monday*, Vol. 15, No. 8, http://firstmonday.org/ojs/index.php/fm/article/
view/3086/2589, 02/08/10.

10. "Teens, Social Media, and Privacy", The Pew Research Center, http://
www.pewinternet.org/Press-Releases/2013/Teens-Social-Media-and-Privacy.
aspx, 21/5/13.

11. "Digital Lives 2010", CHILDWISE, http://www.childwise.co.uk/childwise-
published-research-detail.asp?PUBLISH=64, 2010, p. 56.

12. "Interacting with Children and Young People Online: Part 2: Risk, Privacy
and Consent", BBC, http://www.bbc.co.uk/guidelines/editorialguidelines/
page/guidance-children-interacting-privacy

13. "Monitoring Software", *CNet*, http://download.cnet.com/windows/
monitoring-software/

14. "The parents who police the online bullies", Lucy Cavendish, *The
Telegraph*, http://www.telegraph.co.uk/technology/facebook/8181621/The-
parents-who-police-the-online-bullies.html, 05/12/10.

15. "10 Things Parents Do On Social Media That Embarrass Their Kids",
Callie Harris, *uKnowKids*, http://info.uknowkids.com/blog/bid/293472/10-
Things-Parents-Do-On-Social-Media-That-Embarrass-Their-Kids, 22/5/13.

16. http://www.huffingtonpost.com/sue-sanders/lizzie-wants-to-be-friends-
on-facebook_b_3231129.html?utm_hp_ref=parents-families-tech

17. "Parents Slapped With Stalking Order After Tracking Daughter's Phone",
Chance Kinney, *Mashable*, http://mashable.com/2012/12/28/aubrey-ireland-
stalking-order, 28/12/12.

18. "2013 Best Internet Filter Software Reviews and Comparisons", *TopTen
Reviews*, http://internet-filter-review.toptenreviews.com

19. "SafeSearch: Turn On or Off", Google Help, https://support.google.com/
websearch/answer/3220549?hl=en&rd=1

20. "Keeping children under five safe online", *Mumsnet*, http://www.
mumsnet.com/Internet-safety/preschool-children

21. "Parental tools help make the web safer", Will Gardner, http://www.bbc.co.uk/webwise/0/21259412, 04/02/13.

22. "Internet porn: Automatic block rejected", *BBC News Magazine*, http://www.bbc.co.uk/news/uk-politics-20738746, 25/12/12.

23. "Porn filters: 12 reasons why they won't work (and 3 reasons why they might)", Mona Chalabi, http://www.theguardian.com/politics/reality-check/2013/aug/08/porn-filters-evidence-for-against, 08/08/13.

24. "Children are 'upset' by online violence, study finds'", Maggie Brown, *The Observer*, http://www.guardian.co.uk/technology/2013/feb/03/children-upset-online-violence-study, 02/02/13.

25. "Paris Brown: no further action to be taken over Twitter comments", Press Association, *The Guardian*, http://www.theguardian.com/uk/2013/apr/21/paris-brown-no-action-twitter-comments, 21/4/13.

26. "Google's Eric Schmidt: drone wars, virtual kidnaps and privacy for kids", Charles Arthur, http://www.guardian.co.uk/technology/2013/jan/29/google-eric-schmidt-drone-wars-privacy, 29/01/13.

27. "Sharents to Bio-facture: buzzwords for the future", Nione Meakin, *The Guardian*, http://www.guardian.co.uk/technology/shortcuts/2013/mar/18/sharents-bio-facture-buzzwords-future, 18/03/13.

28. "When to Back Off the Social Media Baby Train", Jeana Lee Tahnk, *Mashable*, http://mashable.com/2013/05/22/social-media-babies, 22/05/13.

29. Tapscott, D., *Grown-Up Digital: How the Net Generation is Changing Your World*, 2008, pp. 66–67.

30. "What to Do When Your Kid's Online Rep Goes Awry", Dan Tynan, http://mashable.com/2013/02/22/online-reputation-kid/, 22/02/13.

31. "Request removal of a cached page", Google Help, https://support.google.com/webmasters/answer/1663691?hl=en&ref_topic=1724262

# Chapter 7

1. "71% of Facebook Users Engage in 'Self-Censorship'", Alexis Madrigal, http://mashable.com/2013/04/15/71-of-facebook-users-engage-in-self-censorship, 15/04/13.

2. Leaning, M., *The Internet, Power and Society: Rethinking the Power of the Internet to Change Lives*, Chandos, 2009, p. 55.

3. Buckingham, D., *Youth, Identity and Digital Culture*, MIT Press, 2008, p. 27.

4. "Why I'm not surprised by Inverdale's 'Looker' Comments", Chine Mbubaegbu, http://amibeautiful.co.uk/2013/07/08/why-im-not-surprised-by-inverdales-looker-comments, 08/07/13.

5. "How are young people affected by sexual images in the media?", Expert View: Dr Linda Papadopoulos, Vodafone, http://www.vodafone.com/content/parents/expert-views/how_are_young_people_affected_by_sexual_images_in_the_media.html

6. Trolley, B.C. and Hanel, C., *Cyberkids, Cyber Bullying, Cyber Balance*, Corwin, 2010, p. 134.

7. "What Teens Get About the Internet That Parents Don't", Mim Ito, *The Atlantic*, http://www.theatlantic.com/technology/archive/2013/03/what-teens-get-about-the-internet-that-parents-dont/273852, 08/03/13.

8. "Managing Social Networking for Children", *The Telegraph*, http://bundlr.com/clips/514f00bd7461b93d9600006a, April 2013.

9. "Child's Education – 3 Ways Dads Can Help", Curt Finn, *Playground Dad*, http://playgrounddad.com/3-simple-ways-dads-can-help-with-their-kids-education-its-not-just-field-trips-anymore, 04/10/12.

10. "Randi Zuckerberg: How I Unplug for My Family", Randi Zuckerberg, *Mashable*, http://mashable.com/2013/04/12/randi-zuckerberg-parenting, 12/04/13.

11. "Study: Adults Are Texting While Driving Even More Than Teens", Charlie White, http://mashable.com/2013/03/28/texting-while-driving, 29/03/13.

12. "Students Confess Their Darkest Secrets on Facebook", Camille Bautista, *Mashable*, http://mashable.com/2013/03/19/facebook-confessions, 19/03/13.

# Chapter 8

1. Livingstone, S., *Children and the Internet: Great Expectations, Challenging Realities*, Polity, 2009, p. 26.

2. Turkle, S., *Alone Together: Why We Expect More From Technology, and Less From Each Other*, 2011, p. 181.

3. danah boyd, a social media scholar, youth researcher, and advocate working at Microsoft Research, New York University Media Culture & Communication and the Harvard Berkmann Center for Internet & Society, chooses to write her name with lower-case initials.

4. Buckingham, D., *Youth, Identity and Digital Culture*, MIT Press, 2008, p. 127.

5. Mizuko, I. *et al.*, *Hanging Out, Messing Around, and Geeking Out*, MIT Press, 2009, p. 96.

6. "The Dunbar Number, from the Guru of Social Networks", Drake Bennett, http://www.businessweek.com/articles/2013-01-10/the-dunbar-number-from-the-guru-of-social-networks, 10/01/13.

7. Mizuko, I. *et al.*, *Hanging Out, Messing Around, and Geeking Out*, MIT Press, 2009, p. 94.

8. Mizuko, I. *et al.*, *Hanging Out, Messing Around, and Geeking Out*, MIT Press, 2009, p. 99.

9. Mizuko, I. *et al.*, *Hanging Out, Messing Around, and Geeking Out*, MIT Press, 2009, p. 27.

10. Mizuko, I. *et al.*, *Hanging Out, Messing Around, and Geeking Out*, MIT Press, 2009, p. 88.

11. Mizuko, I. *et al.*, *Hanging Out, Messing Around, and Geeking Out*, MIT Press, 2009, p. 91.

12. *Digital Parenting*: Issue 1, Vodafone, http://www.vodafone.com/content/ parents/digital-parenting/view_all_magazines.html (November 2010).

13. "How Instagram became the social network for tweens", Michelle Meyers, *CNet*, http://news.cnet.com/8301-1023_3-57508430-93/how-instagram-became-the-social-network-for-tweens, 08/09/12.

14. "Turn Off Your Smartphone Camera's GPS to Protect Your Privacy", Christina Bonnington, *Wired* Magazine, http://www.wired.com/ gadgetlab/2013/07/tip-smartphone-camera-gps, 25/07/13.

15. "Envy on Facebook: A Hidden Threat to Users' Life Satisfaction?", Hanna Krasnova1, Helena Wenninger, Thomas Widjaja, and Peter Buxmann, http:// warhol.wiwi.hu-berlin.de/~hkrasnova/Ongoing_Research_files/WI%20 2013%20Final%20Submission%20Krasnova.pdf, March 2013; "Facebook makes you unhappy – study", Reuters, http://rt.com/news/facebook-makes-unhappy-study-528/, 15/8/13.

16. "Why Facebook is Making Us All Green", Hannah Silley, *Threads*, http:// www.threadsuk.com/why-facebook-is-making-us-all-green, 06/06/13.

17. "Instagram's Envy Effect", Shauna Niequest, *Relevant* Magazine, http:// www.relevantmagazine.com/culture/tech/stop-instagramming-your-perfect-life, 04/04/13.

18. "Social Media, Social Lives: How Teenagers View Their Digital Lives", *Common Sense Media*, http://www.commonsensemedia.org/sites/default/files/ research/socialmediasociallife-final-061812.pdf, Summer 2012.

19. "Imagining the Internet: Millennials will benefit and suffer due to their hyperconnected lives", Pew Research Center, http://www.pewinternet.org/~/ media//Files/Reports/2012/PIP_Future_of_Internet_2012_Young_brains_PDF. pdf, 29/2/12.

20. "Megan Meier's Story", Megan Meier Foundation, http://www. meganmeierfoundation.org/megansStory.php

21. "Father of Teen Suicide Victim Issues Emotional Plea", Andrea Smith, *Mashable*, http://mashable.com/2013/04/11/father-suicide-victim, 11/04/13.

22. "Tom Daley Twitter abuse arrest leads to calls to educate people of legal risks", Lisa O'Carroll, http://www.guardian.co.uk/technology/2012/jul/31/ tom-daley-twitter-abuse-arrest, 31/07/12.

23. "Publishers Revel in Youthful Cruelty", Leslie Kaufman, http://www. nytimes.com/2013/03/27/books/bullying-becomes-hot-and-profitable-topic-for-publishers.html, 26/03/13.

24. *Digital Parenting*: Issue 2, Vodafone, http://www.vodafone.com/content/ parents/digital-parenting/view_all_magazines.html (September 2012).

25. Livingstone, S., Haddon, L., and Gorzig, A., *Children, Risk and Safety on the Internet: Research and Policy Challenges in Comparative Perspective*, Polity Press, 2012.

26. "Web trolls preying on children", ITV, http://www.itv.com/news/

story/2013-02-22/youth-charity-launches-campaign-against-internet-trolling-lauren-goodger-caroline-flack-vinspired, 22/02/13.

27. "Young Canadians in a Wired World III: Talking to Youth and Parents about Life Online", MediaSmarts, http://mediasmarts.ca/sites/default/files/pdfs/publication-report/full/YCWWIII-youth-parents.pdf, 2012.

28. Shariff, S. and Churchill, A. H., *Truths and Myths of Cyber-bullying: International Perspectives on Stakeholder Responsibility and Children's Safety*, Peter Lang Publishing, 2009, p. 3.

29. "Schoolgirl hangs herself after she's bullied by online trolls", *Metro*, http://metro.co.uk/2013/04/29/schoolgirl-hangs-herself-after-shes-bullied-by-online-trolls-3696590, 29/04/13.

30. Mizuko, I. *et al.*, *Hanging Out, Messing Around, and Geeking Out*, MIT Press, 2009, p. 109.

31. Shariff, S. and Churchill, A. H., *Truths and Myths of Cyber-bullying: International Perspectives on Stakeholder Responsibility and Children's Safety*, Peter Lang Publishing, 2009.

32. Willard, N., *Cyber-Savvy: Embracing Digital Safety and Civility*, Corwin, 2012, p. 26.

33. Livingstone, S., Haddon, L., and Gorzig, A., *Children, Risk and Safety on the Internet: Research and Policy Challenges in Comparative Perspective*, Polity Press, 2012, p. 147.

34. Stephens, K. and Nair, V., *Cyberslammed: A Digital Pile On*, Smashup Press, 2013.

35. "Dad Rallies Thousands on Facebook in Anti-Bullying Plea", Vignesh Ramachandran, *Mashable*, http://mashable.com/2013/04/15/dad-anti-bullying-Facebook, 15/04/13.

36. Willard, N., *Cyber-Savvy: Embracing Digital Safety and Civility*, Corwin, 2012, p. 41.

37. "Beatbullying: The Model", *Beatbullying.org*, http://www.beatbullying.org/the-model/

38. Shariff, S. and Churchill, A. H., *Truths and Myths of Cyber-bullying: International Perspectives on Stakeholder Responsibility and Children's Safety*, Peter Lang Publishing, 2009, p. 7.

39. "Moral Disengagement in the Perpetration of Inhumanities", Albert Bandura, *Personality and Social Psychology Review*, 1999, 3, 193. http://www.sociology.uiowa.edu/nsfworkshop/JournalArticleResources/Bandura_MoralDisengagement_1999.pdf

40. "The Moral Panic Over Social Networking Sites", Wade Roush, *MIT Technology Review*, http://www.technologyreview.com/communications/17266/?a=f

41. The Byron Review, 2008, p. 54.

42. Trolley, B. C. and Hanel, C., *Cyberkids, Cyber Bullying, Cyber Balance*, Corwin, 2010, pp. 93–94.

43. Livingstone, S., Haddon, L., and Gorzig, A., *Children, Risk and Safety on the Internet: Research and Policy Challenges in Comparative Perspective*, Polity Press, 2012, p. 103.

44. "Next Generation Users: The Internet in Britain 2011", Dutton, W. H. and Blank, G., http://microsites.oii.ox.ac.uk/oxis, Oxford Internet Institute, University of Oxford, 2011, p. 37.

45. "Combating cyber bullying and technology's downside", Janice D'Arcy, *The Washington Post*, http://www.washingtonpost.com/blogs/on-parenting/post/combatting-cyber-bullying-and-technologys-downside/2011/09/18/gIQAYnUNlK_blog.html, 21/09/11.

46. "Chapter 8: Discussion", Sara Batts, "Informing, inviting or ignoring? Understanding how English Christian churches use the internet" (Unpublished PhD), http://phdinprogress.files.wordpress.com/2013/02/ch-8-discussion.pdf, 2013.

# Chapter 9

1. "Cellphones: A Teen's Lifeline to the Internet", Camille Bautista, *Mashable*, http://mashable.com/2013/03/13/teen-cellphone, 13/03/13.

2. "Tablet Sales Projected to Surpass Laptops in 2013, Total PC Sales by 2015", Jacob Kleinman, *Technobuffalo*, http://www.technobuffalo.com/2013/05/28/tablets-to-outshippcs-idc-report, 28/05/13.

3. Buckingham, D., *Youth, Identity and Digital Culture*, MIT Press, 2008, p. 148.

4. "The Child, the Tablet and the Developing Mind", Nick Bilton, *The New York Times*, http://bits.blogs.nytimes.com/2013/03/31/disruptions-what-does-a-tablet-do-to-the-childs-mind, 31/03/13.

5. "Why don't you call your mother?", Finlo Rohrer, *BBC News Magazine*, http://news.bbc.co.uk/1/hi/magazine/7648334.stm, 02/10/08.

6. "Apps and games for children need to entertain – and educate", Stuart Dredge, *The Guardian*, http://www.guardian.co.uk/media/media-blog/2013/jul/07/apps-games-children-entertain-educate, 07/07/13.

7. "Generation M2, Media in the Lives of 8-to-18-year-olds", Kaiser Family Foundation, http://kaiserfamilyfoundation.files.wordpress.com/2013/01/8010.pdf, January 2010.

8. "Parents Pass-Back Mobile Devices to Children But Are Skeptical of Educational Benefits", Joan Ganz Cooney Center, http://www.joanganzcooneycenter.org/press/parents-pass-back-mobile-devices-to-children-but-are-skeptical-of-educational-benefits, 10/11/10.

9. "Techno-toddlers: A is for Apple", Thomas Jones, http://www.guardian.co.uk/technology/2011/nov/18/techno-toddlers-a-for-apple, 18/11/11.

10. "Does App Store Lack Educational Games for Preteens?", Kate Freeman, http://mashable.com/2013/01/08/app-store-lacking-educational-games, 08/01/13.

11. "Parents Pass-Back Mobile Devices to Children But Are Skeptical

of Educational Benefits", Joan Ganz Cooney Center, http://www.joanganzcooneycenter.org/press/parents-pass-back-mobile-devices-to-children-but-are-skeptical-of-educational-benefits, 10/11/10.

12. "13.4 Billion App Downloads, \$2.2 Billion Revenue In Quarter 1 2013", Lim Yung-Hui, *Forbes* Magazine, http://www.forbes.com/sites/limyunghui/2013/04/08/13-4-billion-app-downloads-2-2-billion-revenue-in-quarter-1-2013/, 08/04/13.

13. "Apple UK urged to refund kids' iPad and iPhone app cash, after US lawsuit", Guy Anker, *MoneySavingExpert.com*, http://www.moneysavingexpert.com/news/phones/2013/02/apple-urged-to-refund-kids-in-app-iphone-and-ipad-purchases-after-us-lawsuit, 26/02/13.

14. "Parents told to beware children running up huge bills on iPad and iPhone game apps", Mark King, *The Guardian*, http://www.guardian.co.uk/technology/2013/jan/12/parents-children-in-app-purchases, 12/01/13.

15. http://www.independent.co.uk/life-style/gadgets-and-tech/news/update-bbm-coming-to-android-and-ios-but-who-knows-when-8648103.html

16. The CHILDWISE Trends Report 2012.

17. "The Touch-Screen Generation", Hanna Rosin, http://m.theatlantic.com/magazine/archive/2013/04/the-touch-screen-generation/309250, 20/3/13.

18. "Phone for 4-year-olds launched, kids' groups are unsure", *CNet News*, Joe Svetlik, http://crave.cnet.co.uk/mobiles/phone-for-4-year-olds-launched-kids-groups-are-unsure-50011189, 11/05/13.

19. *Digital Parenting*: Issue 1, Vodafone, http://www.vodafone.com/content/parents/digital-parenting/view_all_magazines.html (November 2010).

20. "Gregory's iPhone Contract", Janell Burley Hofmann, http://www.janellburleyhofmann.com/gregorys-iphone-contract/, 02/10/10.

21. "1993: Meet the First Digital Generation. Now Get Ready to Play by Their Rules", Jerry Adley, *Wired* Magazine, http://www.wired.com/magazine/2013/04/genwired, April 2013.

22. Edgington, S. M., *The Parent's Guide to Texting, Facebook, and Social Media: Understanding the Benefits and Dangers of Parenting in a Digital World*, Brown Books, 2011.

23. "Teenagers and technology: 'I'd rather give up my kidney than my phone'", Jon Henley, *The Guardian*, http://www.guardian.co.uk/lifeandstyle/2010/jul/16/teenagers-mobiles-facebook-social-networking, 16/07/10.

24. "Imagining the Internet: Millennials will benefit and suffer due to their hyperconnected lives", Pew Research Center, http://www.pewinternet.org/~/media//Files/Reports/2012/PIP_Future_of_Internet_2012_Young_brains_PDF.pdf, 29/2/12.

## Chapter 10

1. Livingstone, S., Haddon, L., and Gorzig, A., *Children, Risk and Safety on the Internet: Research and Policy Challenges in Comparative Perspective*, Polity Press, 2012, p. 208.

2. Livingstone, S., Haddon, L., and Gorzig, A., *Children, Risk and Safety on the Internet: Research and Policy Challenges in Comparative Perspective*, Polity Press, 2012, p. 166.

3. "Young people and pornography", Expert View: Dr Heather Wood, Vodafone, http://www.vodafone.com/content/parents/expert-views/young_people_and_pornography.html

4. "Should children be taught that porn is not real?", Vanessa Barford and Nomia Iqbal, *BBC News Magazine*, http://www.bbc.co.uk/news/magazine-20042508, 24/10/12.

5. "Internet addiction: Cybersex and pornography", *Helpguide.org*, http://www.helpguide.org/mental/Internet_cybersex_addiction.htm#Internet_pornography

6. Livingstone, S., Haddon, L., and Gorzig, A., *Children, Risk and Safety on the Internet: Research and Policy Challenges in Comparative Perspective*, Polity Press, 2012, p. 174.

7. "Sex education will always trump web censorship", Dr Brooke Magnanti, http://www.telegraph.co.uk/women/sex/9817973/Sex-education-will-always-trump-web-censorship.html, 22/01/13.

8. Livingstone, S., Haddon, L., and Gorzig, A., *Children, Risk and Safety on the Internet: Research and Policy Challenges in Comparative Perspective*, Polity Press, 2012, p. 174.

9. "Are parents to blame if kids view pornography?", Luisa Dillner, *The Guardian*, http://www.theguardian.com/theobserver/2012/may/29/internet-pornography-children-access-debate, 29/04/13.

10. "Teen cracks AU$84 million porn filter in 30 minutes", Jo Best, *ZDNet.com*, http://www.zdnet.com/teen-cracks-au84-million-porn-filter-in-30-minutes-1339281500/, 27/08/07.

11. "Do you trust the Government's online filters to protect your child from porn?", Sally Peck, *The Telegraph*, http://www.telegraph.co.uk/women/mother-tongue/9758639/Do-you-trust-the-Governments-online-filters-to-protect-your-child-from-porn.html, 20/12/12.

12. "Mumsnet abandons support for anti-pornography web filters", Emma Barnett and Christopher Williams, *The Telegraph*, http://www.telegraph.co.uk/technology/news/8316997/Mumsnet-abandons-support-for-anti-pornography-web-filters.html, 11/02/11.

13. Thornburgh, D. and Lin, H. S., *Youth, Pornography and the Internet*, National Academy Press: Washington, 2002, p. 4.

14. Gardner, D., *Risk: The Science and Politics of Fear*, Virgin Books, 2009.

15. "Children are 'upset' by online violence, study finds", Maggie Brown,

http://www.guardian.co.uk/technology/2013/feb/03/children-upset-online-violence-study, 02/02/13.

16. "Statistics on child sexual abuse", NSPCC, http://www.nspcc.org.uk/Inform/resourcesforprofessionals/sexualabuse/statistics_wda87833.html, July 2013.

17. "Good practice guidance for the moderation of interactive services for children", UK Council for Child Internet Safety, http://dera.ioe.ac.uk/1969/1/industry%20guidance%20%20%20moderation.pdf, 2010.

18. "Disney plans £3m internet safety campaign around Club Penguin", Stuart Dredge, *The Guardian*, http://www.guardian.co.uk/technology/appsblog/2012/jul/04/disney-club-penguin-child-safety, 04/07/12; "Disney's Club Penguin to invest in child safety online", BBC News, http://www.bbc.co.uk/news/technology-18687249, 04/07/12.

19. "Internet giants planning to wipe out child abuse images", Olivia Goldhill, *The Telegraph*, http://www.telegraph.co.uk/technology/Internet/10161714/Internet-giants-planning-to-wipe-out-child-abuse-images.html, 05/07/13.

20. "How police investigators are catching paedophiles online", Louise Tickle, *The Guardian*, http://www.guardian.co.uk/social-care-network/2012/aug/22/police-investigators-catching-paedophiles-online, 22/08/12.

21. "How Social Media Can Reunite Lost Children With Their Families", Zoe Fox, *Mashable*, http://mashable.com/2013/01/25/how-social-media-can-reunite-lost-children-with-their-families, 25/01/13.

22. "Wootch – Powered By QL-Find Technology", *indiegogo*, http://www.indiegogo.com/projects/wootch-powered-by-ql-find-technology, August 2013.

23. Livingstone, S., Haddon, L., and Gorzig, A., *Children, Risk and Safety on the Internet: Research and Policy Challenges in Comparative Perspective*, Polity Press, 2012, p. 152.

24. "A qualitative study of children, young people and 'sexting'", NSPCC, http://www.nspcc.org.uk/Inform/resourcesforprofessionals/sexualabuse/sexting-research-report_wdf89269.pdf, 2012.

25. "Sexting: Your Photo Fate", Tim Woda, *uKnowKids*, http://info.uknowkids.com/blog/bid/293757/Sexting-Your-Photo-Fate, 24/5/13.

26. "'Noodz,' 'selfies,' 'sexts,' etc., Part 1: A spectrum of motivations", Anne Collier, *NetFamilyNews*, http://www.netfamilynews.org/noodz-selfies-sexts-etc-part-1-a-spectrum-of-motivations, 07/05/13.

# Chapter 11

1. "Free speech haven or lawless cesspool – can the internet be civilised?", Josh Halliday, http://www.guardian.co.uk/technology/2012/apr/19/free-speech-haven-lawless-cesspool, 19/04/12.

2. "The Viral-Media Prof Whose Kids Got 1 Million Facebook Likes (and a Puppy)", Rebecca J. Rosen, *The Atlantic*, http://www.theatlantic.com/

technology/archive/2013/01/the-viral-media-prof-whose-kids-got-1-million-facebook-likes-and-a-puppy/267338/, 19/01/13.

3. Creative Commons Licences, http://creativecommons.org

4. "Record £1bn digital sales", ITV, http://www.itv.com/news/story/2013-01-02/digital-downloads-film-music-games/, 02/01/13.

5. "Parents to pay for kids' illegal music downloads", Tom Pullar-Strecher, *Stuff.co.nz*, http://www.stuff.co.nz/technology/digital-living/8588378/Parents-to-pay-for-kids-illegal-music-downloads, 24/04/13.

6. AVG AntiVirus, http://free.avg.com/

## Chapter 12

1. "Kids, Computers and Computer Vision", Gary Heitling, *All About Vision*, http://www.allaboutvision.com/parents/children-computer-vision-syndrome.htm

"Kids and Computer Eye Strain", Christina Williams, *DavisVision*, http://www.davisvision.com/Kids-and-Computer-Eye-Strain/

2. "Computers And Your Child's Vision", Casey Wonnenberg , *Keloland*, http://www.keloland.com/newsdetail.cfm/computers-and-your-childs-vision/?id=147054, 23/04/13.

3. "Ensuring Mental Wellbeing Online", http://www.tavistockandportman.nhs.uk/wellbeingonline, 29/11/11.

4. "Barriers to the Facebook Generation Getting Help and Support Online", Dr Rachel O'Connell, *The Huffington Post*, http://www.huffingtonpost.co.uk/dr-rachel-oconnell/barriers-to-the-facebook-generation_b_2631115.html, 06/02/13.

5. Carr, N., *The Shallows: How the Internet is Changing the Way We Think, Read and Remember*, Atlantic Books, 2011.

6. "Imagining the Internet: Millennials will benefit and suffer due to their hyperconnected lives", Pew Research Center, http://www.pewinternet.org/~/media//Files/Reports/2012/PIP_Future_of_Internet_2012_Young_brains_PDF.pdf, 29/2/12.

7. "California teens accused of drugging parents to get around internet curfew", Amanda Holpuch, *The Guardian*, http://www.theguardian.com/world/2013/jan/03/teens-accused-drugging-parents-internet, 03/01/13.

8. "Toddlers becoming so addicted to iPads they require therapy", Victoria Ward, *The Telegraph*, http://www.telegraph.co.uk/technology/10008707/Toddlers-becoming-so-addicted-to-iPads-they-require-therapy.html, 21/04/13.

"Four-year-old girl is Britain's youngest iPad ADDICT: Shocking rise in children hooked on using smartphones and tablets", Rebecca Seales and Eleanor Harding, *The Daily Mail*, http://www.dailymail.co.uk/news/article-2312429/Four-year-old-girl-Britains-youngest-iPad-ADDICT-Shocking-rise-children-hooked-using-smartphones-tablets.html, 21/04/13.

"U.K. doctor says kids, as young as 4, becoming addicted to iPads", Marcus Hondro, http://www.digitaljournal.com/article/348527, 21/04/13.

9. "Tough cure for China web addicts", Michael Bristow, BBC News, http://news.bbc.co.uk/1/hi/world/asia-pacific/8219768.stm, 27/08/13.

10. Livingstone, S., Haddon, L., and Gorzig, A., *Children, Risk and Safety on the Internet: Research and Policy Challenges in Comparative Perspective*, Polity Press, 2012.

11. "Internet Addiction: The New Mental Health Disorder?", Alice G. Walton, *Forbes* Magazine, http://www.forbes.com/sites/alicegwalton/2012/10/02/the-new-mental-health-disorder-internet-addiction/, 10/02/12.

12. "Social Media, Social Lives: How Teenagers View Their Digital Lives", *Common Sense Media*, http://www.commonsensemedia.org/sites/default/files/research/socialmediasociallife-final-061812.pdf, Summer 2012.

13. Mayfield, A., *Me and My Web Shadow*, A & C Black, 2010, p. 14.

14. Trolley, B. C. and Hanel, C., *Cyberkids, Cyber Bullying, Cyber Balance*, Corwin, 2010, p. 108.

15. *ENUFF PC*, http://www.akrontech.com

16. "Internet Addiction", *Counselling Directory*, http://www.counselling-directory.org.uk/Internet-addiction.html

17. "Turn Off that Device If You Cannot Sleep!", Shaun Jarmen, *Yahoo Voices*, http://voices.yahoo.com/turn-off-device-if-cannot-sleep-8015178.html, 07/03/11.

18. "Texting at night 'disrupts children's sleep and memory'", Judith Burns, BBC News, http://www.bbc.co.uk/news/education-18357215, 08/06/13.

19. "Ensure children sleep: ban mobiles, say teachers", Daniel Hurst, http://www.theage.com.au/digital-life/digital-life-news/ensure-children-sleep-ban-mobiles-say-teachers-20130510-2jdds.html, 11/05/13.

20. "Imagining the Internet: Millennials will benefit and suffer due to their hyperconnected lives", Pew Research Center, http://www.pewinternet.org/~/media//Files/Reports/2012/PIP_Future_of_Internet_2012_Young_brains_PDF.pdf, 29/2/12.

21. Livingstone, S., Haddon, L., and Gorzig, A., *Children, Risk and Safety on the Internet: Research and Policy Challenges in Comparative Perspective*, Polity Press, 2012, p. 29.

22. Trolley, B. C. and Hanel, C., *Cyberkids, Cyber Bullying, Cyber Balance*, Corwin, 2010, quoting Curtis (1992), p. 130.

23. "Social Media, Social Lives: How Teenagers View Their Digital Lives", *Common Sense Media*, http://www.commonsensemedia.org/sites/default/files/research/socialmediasociallife-final-061812.pdf, Summer 2012.

24. "Teenagers and technology: 'I'd rather give up my kidney than my phone'", Jon Henley, *The Guardian*, http://www.guardian.co.uk/lifeandstyle/2010/jul/16/teenagers-mobiles-facebook-social-networking, 16/07/10.

25. "What Captures Your Attention Controls Your Life", Kare Anderson, *Harvard Business Review*, http://blogs.hbr.org/cs/2012/06/what_captures_your_attention_c.html, 05/06/12.

26. "Get Your Toddler Talking", Kathleen M. Reilly, *Parents.com*, http://www.parents.com/toddlers-preschoolers/development/language/toddler-talking, April 2009.

27. "Children and Their Media 2013", Simon Leggett, CHILDWISE, http://prezi.com/6spkttfivlhp/children-and-their-media-2013/, 2013.

28. "Digital toys don't harm or help your children", Fiona MacGregor, *The Scotsman*, http://www.scotsman.com/scotland-on-sunday/scotland/digital-toys-don-t-harm-or-help-your-children-1-2868686, 31/03/13.

"Inaugural lecture: Prof Lydia Plowman", Edinburgh University, http://youtu.be/9Amunghp5lg, 22/03/13.

# Chapter 13

1. Trolley, B. C. and Hanel, C., *Cyberkids, Cyber Bullying, Cyber Balance*, Corwin, 2010, p. 120.

2. "Next Generation Users: The Internet in Britain 2011", Dutton, W. H. and Blank, G., http://microsites.oii.ox.ac.uk/oxis, Oxford Internet Institute, University of Oxford, 2011, p. 37.

3. "The Touch-Screen Generation, Digital Natives, Your Kids!" Leslie Hendry, *The Huffington Post*, http://www.huffingtonpost.com/leslie-hendry/the-touchscreen-generatio_b_3006391.html, 04/03/13.

4. "The Touch-Screen Generation", Hanna Rosin, http://m.theatlantic.com/magazine/archive/2013/04/the-touch-screen-generation/309250, 20/3/13.

5. "Screen use is bad for brain development, scientist claims", Zoe Kleinman, BBC News, http://www.bbc.co.uk/news/technology-22283452, 15/05/13.

6. "The reinvention of the 1950s living room", Ofcom, http://media.ofcom.org.uk/2013/08/01/the-reinvention-of-the-1950s-living-room-2, 01/08/13.

7. "How I gave my family a digital detox: The mother who banned TV, internet and games consoles for six months and transformed her family's lives", Susan Maushart, http://www.dailymail.co.uk/femail/article-1343209/The-mother-banned-TV-Internet-games-consoles-months-transformed-familys-lives.html, 01/01/11.

8. "I'm still here: back online after a year without the internet", Paul Millar, *The Verge*, http://www.theverge.com/2013/5/1/4279674/im-still-here-back-online-after-a-year-without-the-internet, 01/05/13.

9. "E-books could become the norm for children as sales soar", James Hall, *The Telegraph*, http://www.telegraph.co.uk/news/uknews/9551136/E-books-could-become-the-norm-for-children-as-sales-soar.html, 18/09/12.

10. "Children reading more on screen than print, NLT finds", Charlotte Williams, *The Bookseller*, http://www.thebookseller.com/news/children-reading-more-screen-print-nlt-finds.html, 16/05/13.

11. "The Touch-Screen Generation", Hanna Rosin, http://m.theatlantic.com/magazine/archive/2013/04/the-touch-screen-generation/309250, 20/3/13.

12. I found someone else doing the same here: http://www.serenityyou.com/2012/06/activity-sticks.html


## Chapter 14

1. "Some 6.5 Million People Found Angry Birds in Their Stockings", Ina Fried, *AllThingsD*, http://allthingsd.com/20120103/some-6-5-million-people-found-angry-birds-in-their-stockings, 03/01/13.

2. "Does Gamification Help Classroom Learning?", Beth Blecherman, *Mashable*, http://mashable.com/2013/03/08/games-classroom, 08/03/13.

3. "A to shutter the Medal of Honor brand following Warfighter's 'well below expectations' sales", Jeffrey Matulef, *Eurogamer*, http://www.eurogamer.net/articles/2013-01-30-ea-to-shutter-the-medal-of-honor-brand-following-warfighters-well-below-expectations-sales, 30/01/13.

4. "Good practice guidance for the moderation of interactive services for children", UK Council for Child Internet Safety, http://dera.ioe.ac.uk/1969/1/industry%20guidance%20%20%20moderation.pdf, 2010.

5. "About PEGI?", http://www.pegi.info/en/index/id/23

6. Edgington, S. M., *The Parent's Guide to Texting, Facebook, and Social Media: Understanding the Benefits and Dangers of Parenting in a Digital World*, Brown Books, 2011, p. 78.

7. Whitby, P., *Is Your Child Safe Online: A Parents Guide to the Internet, Facebook, Mobile Phones and Other New Media*, Crimson, 2011, p. 114.

8. The Byron Review, 2008, p. 194, p. 19.

9. "1993: Meet the First Digital Generation. Now Get Ready to Play by Their Rules", Jerry Adley, *Wired* Magazine, http://www.wired.com/magazine/2013/04/genwired, April 2013.

10. "Make sure your kids Wii regularly – why you should encourage children to play video games", Derek Brown, the *Sun*, http://www.thesun.co.uk/sol/homepage/fun/gaming/5000805/Make-sure-your-kids-Wii-regularly-why-you-should-encourage-children-to-play-video-games.html, 08/07/13.

11. "A quiet killer: Why video games are so addictive", Mez Breeze, *The Next Web*, http://thenextweb.com/insider/2013/01/12/what-makes-games-so-addictive, 12/01/13.

12. Carr-Gregg, M., *Real Wired Child: What Parents Need to Know about Kids Online*, Penguin Books, 2007, pp. 60–69.

13. "Gamers hired by father to 'kill' son in online games", Zoe Kleinman, BBC News, http://www.bbc.co.uk/news/technology-20931304, 07/01/13.

14. "Research finds that video games hold both risks and rewards for children with Autism", Anthony John Agnello, *Digital Trends*, http://www.digitaltrends.com/gaming/research-finds-that-video-games-hold-both-risks-and-rewards-for-children-with-autism-spectrum-disorders, 22/04/13.

15. "Video Violence Online: Tips for Parents", Caroline Knorr, *Common Sense Media*, http://www.commonsensemedia.org/blog/video-violence-online-tips-for-parents, 12/03/12.

# Chapter 15

1. "Tonight: Is Technology Taking Over Our Lives?", ITV, http://www.itv.com/news/2012-10-18/tonight-is-technology-taking-over-our-lives, 18/10/12.

2. "Connecting the Learning Society: National Grid for Learning", Government Consultation Paper, https://www.education.gov.uk/consultations/downloadableDocs/42_1.pdf, 1995.

3. "The managing editor... on youth representations in media",    Elisabeth Ribbans, *The Guardian*, http://www.guardian.co.uk/commentisfree/2012/jun/03/youth-representations-in-media, 03/06/12.

4. "Digizen", Childnet International, http://www.digizen.org

5. Safer Internet Day, http://www.saferinternet.org.uk

6. Curran, Sheila and Golding, Tyrrell (2012), "Moving from the periphery to the centre: promoting conversation and developing communities of practice in online environments". In "Renewing the tradition: sustaining and sustainable communities through informal education", 9–11 July 2012, Brathay Hall, Cumbria (http://oro.open.ac.uk/34100/2/4B5D6CE3.pdf).

7. "Protecting Yourself Online: What Everyone Needs To Know", Australian Government, http://www.staysmartonline.gov.au/__data/assets/pdf_file/0005/19598/Protect_yourself_online.pdf, 2010.

8. "Protecting Teens from Identity Theft: A Guide for Adults", National Crime Prevention Council, http://www.ncpc.org/programs/teens-crime-and-the-community/publications-1/preventing-theft/adult_teen%20id%20theft.pdf, Undated.

9. "Fake Facebook pages promise free gifts in exchange for 'Likes'", Steven Musil, *CNet News*, http://news.cnet.com/8301-1023_3-57573495-93/fake-facebook-pages-promise-free-gifts-in-exchange-for-likes, 10/03/13.

10. "Alert: Fake 'Unsealed' Product Giveaways on Facebook", http://wafflesatnoon.com/2013/03/08/alert-fake-unsealed-product-giveaways-on-Facebook, 08/03/13.

11. "What is the likely future of Generation AO in 2020?", Pew Internet Research, http://www.elon.edu/e-web/predictions/expertsurveys/2012survey/future_generation_AO_2020.xhtml, 2012.

12. "Wikipedia: Vandalism", Wikipedia, http://en.wikipedia.org/wiki/wikipedia:vandalism

13. "Social media, teens, parents and whether to 'friend'", Janice D'Arcy, *The Washington Post*, http://www.washingtonpost.com/blogs/on-parenting/post/social-media-teens-parents-and-whether-to-friend/2011/11/04/gIQAxRbL5M_blog.html, 09/11/11.

14. "Should You Be a Digital Tattletale?", Nancy Friedman, *Mashable*, http://mashable.com/2013/04/19/digital-tattletale, 19/04/13.

15. "Imagining the Internet: Millennials will benefit and suffer due to their hyperconnected lives", Pew Research Center, http://www.pewinternet.org/~/media//Files/Reports/2012/PIP_Future_of_Internet_2012_Young_brains_PDF.pdf, 29/2/12.

16. Tapscott, D., *Grown-Up Digital: How the Net Generation is Changing Your World*, 2008, p. 61.

17. 38 Degrees, http://www.38degrees.org.uk

18. Enough Food for Everyone If, http://enoughfoodif.org

19. "Social media users rally to help Boston bombing victims", Channel 4 News, http://www.channel4.com/news/social-media-users-rally-to-help-boston-bombing-victims, 16/04/13.

20. "Suspended Coffees", Occupied Marine, https://www.facebook.com/photo.php?fbid=499848240063369&set=a.248065118575017.53607.246310432083819&type=1&theater

21. Tearfund Bloggers Trip, Dr Bex Lewis, http://drbexl.co.uk/tag/tfbloggers-2, February/March 2013.

# Chapter 17

1. "Next Generation Users: The Internet in Britain 2011", Dutton, W. H. and Blank, G., http://microsites.oii.ox.ac.uk/oxis, Oxford Internet Institute, University of Oxford, 2011.

2. *Digital Parenting*: Issue 2, Vodafone, http://www.vodafone.com/content/parents/digital-parenting/view_all_magazines.html (September 2012).

3. "Which voice recorder will best capture my parents' oral history?", Jack Schofield, *The Guardian*, http://www.theguardian.com/technology/askjack/2013/mar/21/which-voice-recorder-capture-parents-history, 21/03/13.

4. The Byron Review, 2010, p. 16.

5. "Why teaching is 'not like making motorcars'", John D. Sutter, CNN, http://bit.ly/9NoI1Z, 17/03/10.

6. Shariff, S. and Churchill, A. H., *Truths and Myths of Cyber-bullying: International Perspectives on Stakeholder Responsibility and Children's Safety*, Peter Lang Publishing, 2009.

7. "The Social Media Surgery is latest Big Society Award Winner", Gov.UK, https://www.gov.uk/government/news/the-social-media-surgery-is-latest-big-society-award-winner, 16/02/12.

8. "Cyber-bullying, Internet Safety and Social Media Surgeries", Steph Clarke, *Podnosh*, http://podnosh.com/blog/2013/04/26/cyber-bullying-internet-safety-and-social-media-surgeries, 26/04/13.

9. Willard, N., *Cyber-Savvy: Embracing Digital Safety and Civility*, Corwin, 2012.

10. "Youth Work and Social Networking Final Research Report", Tim Davies and Pete Cranston, http://blog.practicalparticipation.co.uk/wp-content/uploads/2009/08/fullYouth-Work-and-Social-Networking-Final-Report.pdf, September 2008.

11. "Help – I want to communicate safely", http://www.ccpas.co.uk/keyfacts/

## Chapter 18

1. Mayfield, A., *Me and My Web Shadow*, A & C Black, 2010, p. 6

2. "Navigating Our Global Future", Ian Goldin, *TED*, http://on.ted.com/fbs6

3. http://mashable.com/2013/08/12/facebook-next-yahoo, 2009.

4. "Imagining the Internet: Millennials will benefit and suffer due to their hyperconnected lives", Pew Research Center, http://www.pewinternet.org/~/media//Files/Reports/2012/PIP_Future_of_Internet_2012_Young_brains_PDF.pdf, 29/2/12.

5. "Thinking Digital Conference", http://www.thinkingdigital.co.uk

6. The Byron Review, 2008, p. 64.